THE VOYAGE OF FRANCOIS PYRARD DE LAVAL TO
THE EAST INDIES, THE MALDIVES, THE MOLUCCAS AND BRAZIL

DESCRIPTION OF THE MALDIVES

FRANCOIS PYRARD DE LAVAL
(1570-1621)

THE VOYAGE OF FRANCOIS PYRARD DE LAVAL TO
THE EAST INDIES, THE MALDIVES, THE MOLUCCAS AND BRAZIL

DESCRIPTION
OF THE
MALDIVES

FRANCOIS PYRARD DE LAVAL
(1570-1621)

AS IT APPEARS IN HAKLUYTUS POSTHUMUS
OR
PARCHAS AND HIS PILGRIMS

VOL-IX
PP 503-570

GYAN

Published by

Gyan Publishing House
5, Ansari Road
Daryaganj, New Delhi-110002
Phone: 011-47034999, 9811692060
E-mail: books@gyanbooks.com

Distribution Network
gyanbooks.com
India, USA, Canada, UK, Australia, France

ISBN : 978-81-212-3305-7 (PB)

2nd Impression 2020

Printed at: Gyan Press, Delhi.

To the Reader.

From the tenth Chapter to the end of this Booke, all is of later Intelligence, and added by way of an Appendix.

OUr Countrey-men, in love with the wealth of India, have brought us (I know not how) backe thorow Turkie to Bagdet and Balsara; neither can wee now returne without some review of India: especially of the parts and Ports there before least visited; and wherof later Intelligence hath come to our hands. Such are the Maldives Ilands, of which hitherto wee have taken small notice in our multiforme Peregrinations. Loe heere therefore wee present you them in a French-English Chart (that I may so speake) both for the translation from the French, and because our Author was Piloted by an Englishman, whose name I finde not; who seeking to escape with some others of his wracked Companie, was done to death by the Maldivans. This our Author learning the Language, with long and deare experience learned this which heere hee freely teacheth, and many many more Observations of these and other places in India; out of which I have gathered what I deemed fittest for our purpose.

Chap. XIX.

The Voyage of Francois Pyrard de Laval, to the East Indies (an English-man being Pilot) and especially his Observations of the Maldives, where being Ship-wracked hee lived five yeares. Translated out of French, and abbreviated.

An. Dom. 1601.

A Company of Merchants of Saint Malo, Laval and Vitre, in the yere 1601. set forth two ships to the Indies; one was of the burthen of foure hundred tunne called the Croissant, the other of two hundred, called the Corbin, sent under the command of the Lord of Bardeliere Burgesse of Saint Malo & Francis Grout, Lord of Closneuf, Constable of Saint-Malo, his Lieutenant or Viceadmirall, Captayne of the Corbin. Wee set sayle from Saint Malo with a North-east winde to begin our Voyage the eighteenth of May, 1601. Being not above nine or ten leagues out in the Sea, our Missen mast broke and split in the middle: this was the beginning of our misfortunes. The third of June, we coasted the Iles of the *Canaries.* Canaries. The twelfth and thirteenth of the same month, wee came to the Ilands of Cape Verd. The nine and twentieth of June, wee found our selves in the height of 5. degrees, and saw the North-starre very low: and at the same time, wee perceived the South-starre. In the *Flying Fishes.* same place and height, we saw great quantities of flying Fishes, with wings like to Bats.

The foure and twentieth of August, wee passed the Equinoctiall line, where are very violent heates, and *The Ternados.* unconstant weather, in an instant a marvellous calme, and halfe an houre after very fearefull Thundrings and Lightnings, and impetuous windes. Often they see come afarre off great whirle-winds, which the Marriners call Dragons: If this passeth over their ship it bruiseth them and overwhelmeth them in the waves. When the *Superstition.* Marriners see one come they take new Swords and beate one against the other in a crosse upon the Prow, or [II.ix.1647.] toward the Coast from whence this storme comes, and hold that this hinders it from comming over their ship, and turneth it aside.

English Pylot. The nine and twentieth of August, our Pilot who was an English-man, from the tops saw land ten leagues off: *Anabon.* this was the Ile of Anabon, whither we came the day following, and were there a while courteously entertayned by the Portugals Lords of the Ilands, but after had *Trecherie of Portugals.* treacherously five of our men surprised by them, and one slaine. The sixteenth of October, we went out of the road of this Ile, and on the seventeenth of November, *Saint Helena.* came to the Iland of Saint Helena. The nine and twen- *The Abroilles, shelves toward Brasil.* tieth of the same moneth, wee doubled the Abroilles.

The seven and twentieth of December, wee passed the Cape of Good Hope. The nineteenth of Februarie,

1602. wee cast anchor in the Bay of Saint Augustine, in the Ile of Saint Laurence, where we abode to refresh our selves, untill the fifteenth of May. The three and twentieth of the same moneth, wee came to the Iles of Comorro, where all that had the Scorbuto or other diseases recovered their health, as well because of the good ayre, as of good water and fruits.

Saint Laurence.

Isles of Comorro.

The one and twentieth of June, wee passed the Equinoctiall toward the North Pole. The second of July in the night, wee were miserably ship-wrackt upon the Bankes of the Maldives, where we lay till the day following, when we imbarked our selves in our Gallion: having taken our Swords, Harquebushes, and halfe Pikes, to goe to Land: after great labour wee attayned one of the Iles called Pouladou, but the Inhabitants would not let us land, before they had disarmed us.

Shipwrack on the Maldivæ Islands.

Pouladou.

They ledde us all together into a House in the middest of the Ile, where they gave us Fruits, Cocos, and Limons. Then the Governour of the Ile came to us called Ibrahim, who seemed very aged, he could speake some words of Portuguise, by the meanes whereof he asked us many things: after his people rifled us, and tooke away all that wee brought, saying that it did belong unto the King. Having beene in this Lodging the space of a day, they tooke the Master of our Ship with two Marriners, and convayed them to the King fortie leagues distant in the Iland of Male. The King sent his Brother in law with many Souldiers to our ship-wrackt Vessell, to get what they could.

Male chiefe of the Maldives.

The Kings Brother in law when hee went away, ledde me and two others into the Iland of Paindoüe, where at our first comming the Inhabitants gave us a little food, but when they saw that our companions had money (this money was about five hundred Crownes, which we tooke while wee were in the ship, and the first night we came on Land we buryed in the ground, which they after digged up wanting necessaries, but wee that were in the Ile of Paindoüe had none of it) they tryed by extremitie of

Paindolle.

Miserable famine.

famine to make us to give them some also, for they beleeved we had some. By reason of this evill resolution of the Ilanders to give us nothing without money, wee were brought into great miserie. All that wee could doe, was to gather Periwinckles on the Sea shoare to eate, and sometimes to meet with a dead Fish. This extremitie endured a long time, till that the Inhabitants seeing wee had no money, began to have a little more commiseration on us; we offered our service to them, to doe what they would imploy us about.

He learnes the Language.

I went often with them to the neighbouring Ilands to get Cocos, and sometimes on Fishing, and in recompence of my labour they gave me part of the Fish or Cocos. While wee lived thus, I endeavoured my selfe to learne the Language, which my companions despised. The Commander of the Ile seeing mee so studious of their Language, began to esteeme and favour me. Then there came one called Assaul Ocaounas Calogue, a Grand Signior, to fetch the rest of the Lead of our ship and some Iron Ordnance, and to make search for the Money which the inhabitants of the Ilands had of our men. The Signior of the Ile of Paindoue and the Catibe, with those that affectioned me, presented me to this Signior that came from the King, and commended me to him: this commendation was the cause that the Signior began to favour me: and also because hee saw I could expresse my selfe in their Language, and daily studied to learne it. hee tooke me with him to carrie me to the King.

He is presented to the King.

When wee arrived at Male, hee went presently to the King to render him an account of the Voyage, and among other things failed not to speake of mee to him. In the evening I went into a Court, whither the King was come to see that which was brought from our Ship. I saluted him in the Language, and after the fashion of the Countrey, which pleased him, and gave him occasion to enquire much concerning those things which were brought from the Ship: hee commanded the Signior that brought me, to lodge and entertaine me. The day following, I was busied with relating to the King, the manners and fashions of our people of Europe and of France. Hee made me see the Queenes, who imployed me divers dayes in giving answers to that which they asked me; being curious to understand the Habits, Manners, Marriages, and fashion of our French Dames.

I was about foure or five moneths in good health, and wanted nothing but the exercise of my Religion and my libertie, having all things else to my content. After this, I fell sicke of a hot burning Feaver. There passed not a day but the King and Queenes sent to know how I did, and every houre sent mee delicious viands to eate, and thus I continued a great while. But afterward the King sent me to the Ile of Bandos (a little Ile in sight of Male) *Bandos.* which hath a better ayre then Male, where an experienced [II.ix.1648.] man by the Kings appointment recovered mee. Afterward the King gave me a lodging neere him, and every day rise out of his owne house, and necessarie provisions for my sustenance, hee gave me also a servant and money, and other presents, so that I became somewhat wealthy after the manner of the Countrey. While I thus continued heere (despairing ever to returne into France) I was diligent to enquire of the people, their manners and customes, which heere I have written and particularised.

§. II.

Description of the Maldives, their thirteene Cantons, twelve thousand Iles, Sea-changes, strange Currents, Monsons, Maine-Inlets, blacke boyling Sea, Heate, Seasons, Civilitie, and haire Ceremoniousnesse.

THe Ilands of the Maldives, begin in eight degrees *Scituation.* of the Equinoctial line, on the North-side and end in foure degrees on the South-side. They are of an extraordinarie length, about two hundred leagues, but not above thirtie or five & thirtie leagues in Latitude. *Their distance.* They are distant from the firme land, that is to say, from

Cape Comorin, from Covan and Cochin, one hundred and fiftie leagues. The Portugals reckon that there are foure thousand and five hundred leagues by Sea, to goe thither from Spaine.

Division into 13. Atollons. They are divided into thirteene Provinces, which they call Atollons, which is a naturall partition according to the scituation of the places. Forasmuch as every Atollon is seperated from others, and contaynes in it selfe a great multitude of small Iles; It is admirable to behold, how that each of these Atollons are invironed round with a huge ledge of Rockes. The Atollons are all after a sort circular or ovall, having each of them thirtie leagues, some a little more, some a little lesse, and lye all one at the end of the other: from the North to Susans, they almost touch one another: there are betweene two channels of the Sea, the one large the other exceeding narrow. Being in the middest of an Atollon, you shall see about you a great ledge of Rockes which impale and defend the Iles, *Force of the Sea.* against the impetuousnesse of the Sea. But it is a very fearefull thing even to the most couragious to approach to this ledge, and see the waves come afarre off and breake furiously on every side. For I assure you, as a thing which I have seene a thousand times, that the surge or billow is greater then a House, and as white as Cotton: so that you shall view round about you as it were a very white Wall, especially when the Sea is loftie.

Now within each of these Cantons, is almost an infinite number of Ilands, both smal and great. The Inhabitants *12000. Ilands.* told me, that there are about twelve thousand. But I conjecture that there appeare not so many, and that they say twelve thousand, to note an incredible number, and which they cannot count. It is true that there are an innumerable multitude of small ones, which are as it were Hillockes of sand, all unpeopled. And moreover, the King of the Maldives puts this number in his Titles, for hee is called Sultan Ibrahim dolos assa raltera Atholon; *Kings Title.* that is to say, Ibrahim Sultan, King of thirteene Provinces and twelve thousand Iles.

Which notwithstanding, the currents and daily flowing of the Sea diminish that number, as the Inhabitants informed me, who said also that a proportion of the number of the people are consumed, and that there are not so many as were accustomed to be anciently. Also they reported that within one of the Atollons, all the little Iles and Sea which part them, was one continued ground, and that it was in former times but one only Ile, cut and divided after into many. And surely they which navigate neere the Maldives, discerne all within white, by reason of the sand which is of this colour, upon all the Flats and Rocks. The Sea thereabouts is very quiet and of a meane depth, insomuch that the deepest entrance is not twentie fathomes; and yet heere are very few entrances: for a man may almost see the bottome every where.

Sea makes daily alteration.

All the shallowes are stone, Rocke and sand, so that when the tide is out, it reacheth not to ones waste, and for the most part to the mid-legge; so that it were very easie to goe without a Boate throughout all the Iles of the same Atollon, if it were not for two causes. The one great fishes called Paimones, which devoure men and breake their legges and armes, when they encounter them; the other is that the depths of the Sea are generally very keene and sharpe Rockes which hurt them wonderfully that goe into it. And moreover, they meete with many branches of a certaine thing which I know not whether to terme Tree or Rocke, it is not much unlike white Corall, which is also branched and piercing, but altogether polished; on the contrary, this is rugged, all hollow and pierced with little holes and passages, yet abides hard and ponderous as a stone. They call it in their Language Aquiry, they keepe it to make their Honey and Sugar of Cocos, having bruised them with little stones, and putting them to boyle with the water of Cocos, this is that which fashions their Honey and their Sugar. It greatly hinders those which wash themselves in the Sea, it was very difficult to me to goe so from Ile to Ile without a Boate, but they which are accustomed goe often.

Danger by Sharkes and sharpe stones.

A kind of Currall.

[II.ix.1649.] *Many of the Ilands are not inhabited.* Amongst these Ilands there are very many, and as I beleeve the greatest number, which are wholly unhabited, and which have neither Trees nor Herbs; others which have no greene thing, and are but a moveable sand: yet there are some which are for the most part overflowne at spring tides, and are discovered when the Sea is out, the residue are all covered with great Crabs (which they call Cacouve) and Cray-fishes.

Prodigious numbers of the Pinguy Fowles. There are great store of Fowles called Pinguy, which heere lay and hatch, and here is such a prodigious multitude of them, that a man knowes not (I have often made triall) where to set his foot without touching their Egges, or young ones, or the old Birds, which flye not farre when they see men. The Ilanders eate them not, and yet they are very good meate, and as bigge as Pidgeons, their Feathers white and blacke. These Iles which I have said to bee unhabited, appeare afarre off white, as if they were covered with Snow, by reason of the great whitenesse of the Sand which is fine and subtle, as that of an Houre-*Heat of sands.* glasse, and so hot and burning, that the Egges of those Birds are hatched with great facilitie.

Want of water. They have great scarcitie of fresh water, some Ilands are well woodded and inhabited which have not any; except some few, whither the Inhabitants are constrayned to go and seeke it from the confining Iles; also they have inventions to receive raine water: and although they have water in the Iles, they are not like one another; being better in one respect then another. All their Pit-water *Pits how made.* is neither very sweet nor wholsome. They make their Pits in this manner, digging three or foure foot in the Earth, a little more or lesse, they find fresh-water in abundance, and (that which is very strange) not above foure feet from the Sea-shore, in places also which are *Hot at night and cold at noone.* often over-flowne. I have observed that their waters are very cold in the day, principally at noone, and in the night very hot.

But to returne to the thirteene Atollons, here are their names beginning at the North Point, which is in the head, which the Portugals call for that cause Cabexadel las ilhas, and in the Maldives Tongue, Tilla dou matis, in the same signification, that is to say, the high Point, which is under eight degrees of the Line on the North-side, in the same height that Cochin is. Now the first Atollon is called Tilla dou matis. The second Milla doue madoue. The third, Padypolo. The fourth, Malos madou. The fift, Ariatollon. The sixt, Male Atollon, which is the principall where is the Iland of Malé, chiefe over the others. The seventh, Poulisdous. The eighth, Molucque. The ninth, Nillandous. The tenth, Collo madous. The eleventh, Adou matis. The twelfth, Souadou. The thirteenth, Addou and Poua Molucque, which are distinguished into two little ones, and separated, as the others, but are very small, and therefore are accounted as one. Notwithstanding, Addou, as the better, gives name to the other.

Names of the Atollons.

Every Atollon is separated from his Neighbour by a channell of the Sea, which passeth betweene them. But although they cannot passe with great ships without perishing, yet there are foure which are farre larger then the others, and may easily passe for great ships, notwithstanding, it is very dangerous, and perillous to goe here, and especially in the night: for it is certaine to bee shipwrackt (as we were) because they cease not to encounter certaine Shoalds and Rockes, which they ought to shunne. I have seene amongst the Maldives many Sea-cards, where these were exquisitely deciphered. These people also are marvellous cunning to avoide them, and to saile through passages very dangerous without perishing. I have seene them often passe in the middle of the Bankes, Sands, and Rockes, through little channels so narrow, that they had roome only for their Barke, and sometimes so evenly that they grated the Rockes on both sides; and neverthelesse they went securely in the middest of those perils, and with a high saile. Once being with some of the Ilanders in a little Boate, which was not above foure fathome long, the Sea was higher then I two Pikes length,

Foure principall channels.

The Native. dexteritie in sayling.

and so outragious and turbulent as could not be more. I thought every moment that the billow would have carried mee out of the Boat; where I had great labor to hold my selfe, and they were not a whit perplexed, nor did feare any thing. For they feare not the Sea, and are very skilfull to conduct Barkes and Boats, being made and accustomed to this from their youth, aswell the Gentlemen as poore people, and it should be a disgrace to them to be ignorant in it. For this cause it is impossible to summe up the number of Barkes and Boates which are throughout all the Iles, for as much as the poorest will have one, the rich many. They never saile by night, but take Land every evening, they saile not neither without sight of Land without a Compasse, except when they goe out of their Iles, and goe some long Voyage. They carrie therefore little provision, but buy daily whatsoever they need in divers Islands.

Numberlesse number of Barkes.

No sayling by night.

Shoalds.

The greatest part also of the Iles which are within the circuite of one Atollon, are surrounded with a shoald, and there are but one or two open places which are very strait and difficult to heed: wherefore it is necessary that they understand well the manner actively to guide their Barkes: otherwise if they be defective the least thing in the World, their Barke will bee overwhelmed, and their Merchandize perish. As for the men they can swimme well, which in those parts of the Sea preserves them daily, and to speake truly, they are as it were halfe fishes, they are so used to the Sea, whither they goe daily either swimming, or roading or waling. I have seene them many times within the ledge of Rockes where the Sea is
[II.ix.1650.] calme, runne swimming after the fishes, which they have suddenly perceived bathing themselves, and have taken them in their course. And this is usuall. And yet they faile not often to lose their Barkes, notwithstanding all their dexteritie.

Good Swimmers.

Strange Sea-currents.

The greatest discommoditie is the current Pyvarou, which run aswell to the East as the West, in the channels of the Iles, and in divers in-draughts of the Sea, six moneths on one Coast, and six months on another; yet not certainly, but sometimes more, sometimes lesse. This is that which deceives them, and ordinarily casts them away. The winds are aswel fixed as the currents, from the East quarter or the West, but they vary sometimes, and are not so ruled, fetching their Compasse toward the North or the South, and the current goes perpetuall his accustomed course, till the season alter. It is a very remarkable thing, that whereas the Atollons are continued one at the end of the other, and separated by channels of the Sea which goe thorow them, they have open places and entrances opposite one to the other two on one side, and two on the other, by which meanes men may goe and come from Atollon to Atollon, and alway communicate together. Wherein may be observed an effect of the providence of God, which hath left nothing unperfect. For if there were but two open places in every Atollon, that is, one on one side, and another on the other; it were not possible to passe from Atollon to Atollon, nor from entrance to entrance, because of the boysterousnesse of the currents; which runne sixe moneths to the East, and sixe to the West, and permit not to crosse over, but force them downe. And when the two entrances are not adverse, but one on the East Coast, the other on the West, men may easily enter, but not returne, except the sixe monethes are ended, and the current changed. Now as these entries are disposed, men may notwithstanding the currents goe from one Atollon to another, in every season, and Traffique, and Merchandize freely together, as they doe; for as much as every Atollon is open with foure entrances which are in opposition to their two Neighbours.

The Monsons.

Inlets opposite.

The entrances of these Atollons are unlike, some competently broad, others very narrow, the largest is not more then two hundred paces or thereabouts; some are but thirtie, nay lesse. On both the sides of each of these passages are two Iles, on each side one; you would say that it were to guard the comming in, which surely were

Forme of the Entrances and their danger.

easie to doe, if they would, with Ordnance hinder the ships to enter, because the largest hath not above two hundred paces. Now concerning the channels (which they call Candou) which divide the Atollons, foure are Navigable, where the great ships may goe to passe through the Maldives, many strangers ships of all sorts passe often there, but not without perill, for there are a great number yeerely cast away. It is not that they affect this passage (for all on the contrary shunne it, as much as may be) but they are situated in such sort in the middest of the Sea, and so long, that it is not easie to escape them, principally the currents carrie the ships thither against their wils, when the calmes or contrary winds take them, and that they cannot helpe themselves with their sailes, to make way against the currents. The first beginnes on the North-side, and is that where wee were shipwrackt at the entry of the shelfe of the Atollon of Malos madou. The second approacheth very neere Malé, called Caridou, in the middest whereof is the greatest of all the Iles, so hemmed in with Rocks as I have said. The third, is by Malé, stretching towards the South, and is called Addou. The fourth, is called Souadou, which is directly under the Equinoctiall Line: this is the greatest of all, having more then twentie leagues in widenesse.

The first.

The second, third, and fourth.

The Ilanders going by the Iles and Atollons, helpe not themselves with a Compasse, except in farre Voyages, but when they passe through the great channell they use it. All the other channels betweene the Atollons are very straite, and full of Rockes and Shoalds, they cannot goe but in small Barkes, and yet it is requisite to have great knowledge of the places to saile without danger. I found it strange sayling with the Ilanders in the channell, which separates Malé and Polisdou, and which beares the name of Polisdou, and is seven leagues broad or thereabouts, that the Sea appeares there blacke as Inke, notwithstanding beeing taken up in a Pot, it differs not from other water; I saw it daily boyle in bigge blacke billowes, as if it had beene water on the fire. In this entrance the

No Compasse but in long Voyages.

Sea blacke as Inke; the water not.

Sea runnes not as in other places, which is fearefull to behold: I thought I was in the nethermost depths perceiving not that the water mooved on one side or the other. I know not the reason, but I know well that the Natives are greatly afraid of it: they very often encounter such tortures.

Seeing these Iles are so neere the Equinoctiall on both sides, it may bee judged what is the qualitie of the Aire, which is very intemperate, and the heate excessive. Notwithstanding the day and night are alwayes equall, the nights are very coole, and bring abundance of dew. This coolenesse is a cause that the Countrey may bee more commodiously inhabited, and that the Herbs and Trees are fruitfull, notwithstanding the heate of the Sunne. The Winter beginnes in the moneth of Aprill, and continues six monethes and the Summer in the moneth of October, which endures sixe other moneths. The Winter is without Frost, but alwayes rainie. The Winds are violent from the West Coast; on the contrary the East is extreame hot, and never causeth raine.

Heat. *Dewes.* *Winter.* *Winds.*

They affirme, that the Maldives have beene heretofore peopled by the Cingala, (so they call the Inhabitants of the Iland of Ceylan.) But I finde that the Maldives resemble not at all the Cingala, which are blacke, and very evill featured, and these are well shaped and proportioned, and little differ from us, except their colour, which is Olive. But it is out of doubt, that the place and the length of time have made them more gracefull then those which first inhabited the Iles. Adde also that there are seated a great number of strangers of all parts, which inhabit there, (besides the Indians) who from time to time have been shipwrackt as we were. Wherefore the people which inhabit Malé, and round about to the North point are found more orderly, honest and civill: and they which are on the South-side toward the low point, are more rude in their Language and Fashions, and not so well featured; and blacker, and also many women of the poorer sort are naked without any shame,

Whence peopled. [II.ix.1651.] *Civilitie of the North parts.* *South barbarous.*

having only a little cloth to cover their Privities: And for as much as the North-coast is daily more haunted and frequented with strangers who ordinarily marrie there: Also that it is the passage of all the ships, which enrich the Countrey, and civilize it more and more, which is the cause that persons of ranke and qualitie seate themselves there more willingly, and not toward the South, whither the King sends in Exile those which he will punish with banishment. And yet the people which inhabit the South parts, are not inferiour in capacitie or Religion to the others, if it be not more for other things, but all their Gentry inhabit on the North Coast, where also they take their Souldiers.

Religion. The people are very Religious, greatly addicted to Manufactures of all kindes of Workes, wherein they excell, also in Letters and Sciences after their manner, principally in Astrologie, whereof they make great esteeme. They are a wise and circumspect Nation, very fradulent in their Merchandizing, and their living in the World. They are valiant and hardie, and well seene in Armes, and live in great order and policie. *Women.* The women are faire, but that they are of an Olive colour: and some are found as white as they be in Europe, yet they have all blacke haire: *Haire-ceremonies.* but they esteeme that beautie, and many make it to come so, wherefore they keep their Daughters heads shaven, till the age of eight or nine yeeres, not leaving them till then any haire but a little on their fore-heads, to distinguish them from Boyes, who have none at all, yet this comes not lower then their Eye-browes, and after that the children are borne, they shave them from eight dayes to eight dayes, which makes their haire very blacke, that would not be so else, for I have seene little children with halfe flaxen haire.

The beautie and ornament of the women is to have their haire very long, thicke, and blacke, which they accommodate and wash often, and purifie with water and *Bathing and Oyling.* Lye made of purpose: having well washed and clensed their heads and haire, they abide in the wind all dishevelled, but within the compasse of their house, untill it bee throughly dry; after they rub and oyle their haire with odoriferous Oyle, which causeth that their heads are alwayes moyst and Oily. For they never wet their bodies men nor women, but after they oyle them, two or three times in the weeke for their haire, but for their bodie, oftener then there are dayes. As for their haire they are not obliged to wash it, but when they have accompanied together, and they are bound particularly every Friday, which is their Sabbath, and in all their great Feasts; the men on their Fridayes, the women on their severall Feasts only, but sleepe after it when they shall thinke good and according to their necessitie. The women also perfume their heads for a little reason which they have, and so washed, oyled, and perfumed they attire themselves, which is to bring all their haire from before backward, and draw it out as much as may be, that one haire may not move nor waver this way nor that way: after they tye them behind, or they make a great tuft bound on, for which greatnesse, they have a counterfeite Locke of mans haire, but as long as the womens, in fashion of a Horse taile; and to hold it, they garnish it at the great end after the manner of a ([l]) and all the rest of their haire is put in order: after the ([m]) of Gold or Silver is covered with Pearles and Jewels according to their abilities: and some weare two of these false haires, because it serveth to tye their haire behind, and make the tuft greater. They put also odoriferous flowers of the Countrey, which is not thereof defective.

[l] *De dez a coudre.*
[m] *Dez.*

It is not permitted the men, but onely the Souldiers and Officers of the King, and Gentlemen to weare their haire long, who doe so for the most part, and as long as the womens, yea take as much paines as they to wash, clense, and oyle and sweeten it with flowers: and there is no other diffrence, but that the men bind their haire on one of their sides, or right up, or upon the head, and not behinde as the women: also they never weare any false Periwigs: they are not compelled to weare their haire so, but short or long, as they thinke good. I have seene the King and the Princes, and greatest part of the Grandes and Souldiers, who weare their haire short, and they which weare them long, for the most part, when they are weary, or when they grow no more, cut them off to give or sell to women, for they have no counterfeit haire, but mens, because they never shave the womens haire living or dead: the most part of these false haires come from the Continent, as from Cochin, Calicut and all the Coast of Malabar, where all the men weare their haire long, which after they cut and sell for women, as wel of the Countrey as Aliants. Their haire increaseth there a great deale faster then here, because, as I conjecture, they so often wash and oyle them, also by reason of the extraordinary heate, which causeth their haire to be thicker and harder, but never curled as with us. Commonly also the men are hairy over all the bodie, yea so thicke as more cannot be imagined; hereof they boast, as if it were the strength of nature; which yet they finde not alwayes true, and if a man bee not so hairy, they say, that hee rather resembles a woman then a man, and despise him for it: but the women are not so hairy, and have no haire but in ordinary places.

Increase of haire.

Hairie on their bodies.

[II.ix.1652.]

All Barbers and none.

There is no common Barbers, but every one hath skill to shave, as well men as women, and to use no razor for it, nor any combe; but they have sizers of cast copper, and looking-glasses also of copper, which they use instead of razors of steele, but not made as ours. They shave themselves after our fashion: for the King and Peeres, there are men which account themselves honoured to serve in this office, not for gaine, but for affection, being men of fashion; the King sends them presents at the yeeres end. Also throughout all the Ilands there is neither man nor woman, rich nor poore, great nor little, which after the age of fifteene yeeres hath not all their furniture and instruments so to order their head: and they are very curious to take them off when it never so little grieves or troubles them.

The maidens weare no coats till the age of eight or nine yeeres, but onely a cloth which reacheth from the girdle to the knee, which they weare from the time they begin to goe: but the boyes weare nothing till they are seven yeeres olde and are circumcised: they say that it is not necessary that their daughters should weare any other robe the time aforesaid, for that then their breasts begin to beare out & increase, and it is needfull to cover them, as a thing which they hold as great a shame to show, as here their privities; and then they let their haire increase without any more cutting, but adorne and trim it, being then in the time to finde some to marry with; for before that they hold them as children, and permit not men nor boyes to speake of love to them, for that they are not acknowledged nor arrayed as maidens. Now the men being very old and covered with haire, as I have said, and not clothing their bodies from the girdle upwards, they shave not the haire on the breast and stomacke, but in such a fashion as they cut the haire in one place, and leave it in another, to the end that it may appeare and bee like the fashion of a cased doublet.

Boyes and girles.

Shame to let the breasts be seene.

The men weare their beards in two fashions: one which is permitted to the Pandiares, Naibes, and Catibes, and other Ecclesiasticall persons, and those which have gone on pilgrimage to Mecca, and Medinatalnaby in Arabia, where is the Sepulchre of Mahomet, to weare their beard so long as they will, and not to shave it but under the throat, and their upper and lower lips, because they would not for any thing being eating or drinking touch a haire, being the greatest nastinesse and filthinesse in the world: wherefore they have no haire about their mouth; and I have often seene that for finding onely one haire in a platter of meat, they would not touch it, and remained rather without eating, giving it to the birds and other creatures, except any bodie would have it. The other sort of beards for the rest of the nation, and the commonest is to weare a little one after the Spanish custome, shaven about their mouth and under their throat, but

Beards of two sorts.

Neat superstition.

Curiositie.

without mustaches, and in the cheekes they make like holes and fashions with the sizers, and they shave them very close, yet so that it may appeare. Their chin as we use now.

Very niggards. In the meane while they curiously keepe the shavings of their haire and nailes, without losing or letting fall any, and are carefull to interre it in their Church-yards with a little water: for they would not for any thing in the world goe upon it, or cast the lest part into the fire; because, they say, being part of the bodie it requires burying as wel as the bodie; and they inclose it neatly in a little cotton, and the most of them wil be shaven in the porches of their temples or Moschees. They are verie hardie and insensible in all this, and use no hot water in shaving them; their razors cut verie naughtily, and they doe nothing but poure a little cold water upon it; and whatsoever hurt they do, they complaine not, and say that it paines them not: All this comes of custome to them, for else they would be as sensible as we.

§. III.

Their Cocos and other fruits and food, their Trades and trading, Creatures profitable and hurtfull. Of Male the principall Iland. Their Houses, Candou, Languages, Apparell.

THe Maldives are very fertill, fruit, and other commodities necessarie for the life of man. They have abundance of Millet, which they call Pura, also of another little graine called Bimby, which is like to Millet, but that it is blacke as Rape-seed. These graines sow themselves, and are reaped twice in a yeere. They make a kinde of meale, whereof they make pottage with milke and hony of Cocos, and also of Torteaux and Bignets, and many other sorts of food. There grow also rootes of many kindes, one called Itelpoul, which growes in abundance without sowing, and is round, and

Their food Millet.

two handfulls in greatnesse, little more or lesse. Now they bruise it by rubbing it on a rugged stone: after they lay it in a cloth in the Sunne to dry, this is like our Amidon or wheate-flower, which they keepe as long as they wil, whereof they make pottage, and Torteaux and Gullets, which is a verie delicate meat, but that it a little surchargeth the stomacke, it must bee eaten while it is [II.ix.1653.]
new. They have plentie of another sort of root, called *Roots.* Alas, of a very good taste, which they sow and cultivate, one sort red, like red-parsnip, another white like navews, and are ordinarily bigger then a mans thigh. They boile and dresse them in divers fashions, and keepe them a great part of the yeere; also they order them with hony and sugar of Cocos, and it is a great part of the nourishment of these people. They call wheat Godame & rice Andove, which grows not there, but is brought in great quantitie from the firme land. They eat and prepare it in divers manners, boyling it only with water, and eat it with other viands in stead of bread. They boyle it also, after dry it and bray it, and of this bran, with egges, hony, milke, and butter of Cocos, they make Florentines, and verie good belly-timber.

Hearbs, trees, and fruits. Hearbes and trees grow plentifully in all the Iles; many that beare fruit, others that beare none, whereof notwithstanding they eate the leaves which are sweet and daintie. There are Citrons, Pomgranets, Orenges in abundance; Bannanes, which the Portugalls call figges of India, and the Maldives Ouella, which is a great fruit, and multiplies exceedingly, delicious and of great nourishment; so that they nourish their infants with it in stead of broth. There is none more profitable then the Cocos or nut of India, which they call Roul, and the *Cocos.* fruit Cate: they abound more in the Maldives then in any place of the world: this onely tree serves for all necessaries of life, furnishing them in great quantitie with wine, hony, sugar, milke, and butter; and moreover the pith or kernell serves to eate, with all sorts of meate in stead of bread. Adde also the wood, barke, leaves, and shells make the greatest parts of their moveables and utensills.

There is such store of fire-wood, that they buy it not, for as much as the countrie is covered with all sorts of *Trees common.* trees: it is lawfull to goe and cut those trees at any time when they have need, which serve for nothing but to burne. Also there are whole Ilands full, whither everie one send their servants and slaves daily to fetch for their use. It is admirable that each of the thirteene Atollons produce sundry fruits, although they are all under the same climate; yet every one hath not that which is necessarie. You would say, that God would that these people should visite one another, here is such diversitie: for what is plentifull in one place is rare in another. Although every thing growes particularly in each place, yet it is little, and not so good and naturall as that which comes from the Atollons and Iles proper to it, because it is brought from other places.

The people also have followed in their habitations a *Crafts differing with the Ilands.* like order, for the crafts-men are assembled in Iles apart, as the Weavers in one, the Gold-smiths in another, and so all the rest. In briefe, none of their mechanick Arts are mingled, but each hath his Ile, yet they communicate one with another in this sort: they have close boates, with a little deck, and goe from Ile to Ile travelling and retayling their merchandize, and sometimes are more then a yeere before they returne to their Ile and ordinarie residence. They carrie with them their male children, from foure or five yeere old, to learne and be accustomed to it. They lye alwayes in their Barkes, and drinke and eate there, and often worke also. When I was on the Maldives, there was found a Bird (which landed in an Iland) of prodigious shape and greatnesse. It was three foot high, the body exceeding great, more then a man could fathom: the feathers all white as a Swan, the feet broad like Fowles that swim, the necke halfe a fathom long, the beake halfe an ell; on the upper part at the end a kinde of crooked claw, underneth larger then above, whence hung a very great and capable bagge of a yellow gilded colour resembling parchment. The King was much astonished whence this creature should come, and what was the nature of it: and enquiring of all men which came from other regions, at the last hee happened on certaine strangers, who told him that this creature was particular to China, and that it was bred no where else, and that the Chinois use them to take fish, for this creature swimmeth on the water as other river Birds, and very long. It takes fish with great dexteritie, and fills the great purse or bagge which hangs from the beake underneath, which is so great and capable, that it will hold many fishes each two feet long, which the King handling hard, wondred greatly how it was possible that this Bird should come so alone from China, being distant more then a thousand and two hundred leagues. The King made triall, causing them to tye and fasten his throat, onely giving it leave to breath, that it might not swallow the fish, but bring up the poke full. I have seene it often goe so on the Sea, and come with it full of fish. It goeth a long time on the Sea, and tarries there sometimes a day, which makes me beleeve that it is not impossible that it should come from China.

They have Hens in such plentie, that it is strange, and cost them nothing but the taking, for they are wild: in the Market they sell them but for one Sous apiece, and thirtie sixe Egges at the same price; this is the meate they use most next to fish. They have store of Pidgeons, of Duckes, of Rayles, and of certayne Birds which altogether resemble Sparrow-hawkes, Muskets blacke and gray, which live not of prey, but of fruits and many other differing kinds, all wilde and none domesticke. The Crowes greatly indanger the Inhabitants; for they are so bold, that they will come into the Houses; and take any thing, although men be present, of whom they are not awhit afraid. At the first, I thought they had been tame and domesticall, they are in so great abundance that they cannot be numbered, because they kill them not. The

Hens wilde. *Other Fowle.* *Crowes bold.*

Great Bats. Muskitos, Rats, Mice, Pismires, &c. [II.ix.1654.] *Of these creatures see Linschot. C. 45. who relateth the like in Goa.*

Bats are as great as Ravens. They are greatly annoyed by the Muskitos or Gnats, which pricke very sorely. But that which troubles them most are the Rats, Dormice, and Pismires which are found every where, with other sorts of Creatures and Vermine which enter into their Houses, and eate and spoyle their Graine, Provision, Fruits, and tender Commodities, so that they are forced for to resist them, to build their Lodges and Granaries on piles in the Sea two and three hundred paces from the Land, whither they goe in Boates, and there lay up their graine and fruits to keepe them. The most part of the Magazines of the King are builded after this manner.

Sea-snakes.

In the Sea there is a kinde of Snakes which are very dangerous. There are great store of Cats, Foines, and Ferrets. There are no beasts for riding; there are few great beasts, wilde or tame. It is true that there are about foure or five hundred Cowes and Bulls: but they appertaine to the King onely who breeds them in the Ile of Male: whither they are brought from the firme land for curiositie to multiply to that number; They eate them not, but in foure or five months in the yeere, and at great feasts when the King causeth to kill one, and sometimes he giveth one to the strangers ships, whom hee will gratifie. There are also some Weathers which are the Kings. They have no Dogges, yea are greatly afraid of them. While that I was there, the Portugalls of Cochin sent two to the King for a raritie, who caused them incontinently to be drowned. If any touch a Dogge, he presently goes to bath, as to purifie himselfe.

Dogs dreadful and uncleane.

Fish.

The Sea is very full of fish, of all sorts great and small, principally because it is shallow and calme within the Atollons. It is their chiefe sustenance, either fresh with Rice or other meate, or fried with Oyle of Cocos, or sod in sea-water and dryed to keepe it. They send many ships daily laden to Achen in Sumatra and other places. There is one great kinde of fish which greatly vexeth them, for it devoures the men when they bath or go a fishing. I escaped very hardly from being devoured. A

Sharkes.

man may see a great number of persons which have lost their armes or legges, or otherwise are lamed by this misfortune. The great abundance of all things causeth that victuall costs little, and that every thing is good cheape. Foure hundred Cocos may bee bought for one Larin, which is eight souses: five hundred Bannanes for one Larin: in like manner after the same price an hundred great fishes, or a dozen of good Hens, or three hundred pound of Roots, and so of other things: so that there is no * Country in India where strangers grow rich so soone, because trading is good, and victualls cheape.

Cheape victuall.

**Note.*

The principall Iland is called Male, which gives name to all others: for the word Dives signifieth a number of small Iles heaped together: it is very neere the middest of all other Iles, and is in circuit about a league and a halfe. It is fruitfuller then all the rest, and the Staple and Mart of them, and of strangers; the seat of the King and of the Court. By reason whereof it is best peopled, but unhealthfullest; there dye many, whom they interre each a part, so that all the Ile is full; the Sunne, which is very hot, draweth up noysome and pestilent vapours. The waters also are naught, the King therefore is compelled to send, for him and his house, to another Ile, where the water is better, and where they bury no bodie; so doe also the principall and men of abilitie in the Ile. Throughout all the Ilands they have no enclosed Townes, no not in the Ile of Male. But all the Ile is replenished here and there with houses and buildings, either of Lords and Gentlemen, or of the common people, and also of others. Notwithstanding the houses are distinguished by Streets and Wards, in a faire order, and all know their owne division. The houses and edifices of the common people are of Wood of the Cocos, which they cut from the trunke of the Tree, they cover them with leaves of the same Tree, sowed double one within another.

Male the principall Iland.

Unhealthfull.

No walled Townes.

Their houses.

The Signiors and rich men build with stone, which they draw forth of the Sea, from under the Shelfs and Rockes, where they find as much as they will, of good

Sea-stones how drawne thence.

length and greatnesse. It is smooth and good merchandise, verie white, somewhat hard to cut and fashion: but assoone as it raines on it, it loseth its naturall hardnesse and whitenesse, and becomes all blacke when it is beaten with the raine, or wet with fresh water: the manner of drawing them forth of the Sea is remarkable. There groweth in that Countrey a kind of Wood which they call Candou, which is as great as the Wall-nut tree here, like in the shaking leafe, and whitenesse, but wonderfull soft. It beares not any fruit, and is fit onely to burne: being dry they cut it into Plankes, which they use as we doe fire. This Wood is lighter then Corke. Having noted the stone within the water which they will have, they fasten it with a great Cable. This is ordinary, for as I said before, they are halfe fishes, very expert in swimming, their women swim as well or better then the men of these parts: so that they will goe on every occasion to the bottome of the Sea, fifteene or twenty fathoms deepe, and stay there a long time and marke the depths very often, to see where it is good laying their anchor. Sometimes also in stead of an anchor they choose some great rocke in the bottome of the Sea, and there fasten their Cable. Then after that they have selected the stone, which they will draw up, & that they have bound it to their Cable, they take a piece of the wood of Candou, & tie or thrust through (after they have bored it) their cable right opposite to the stone, and after aloft adde a certaine number of these pieces, as many as shall be necessary, so that which is marvellous light, and fleeting above the water, pulls up with it the stone and draweth it aloft, whatsoever weightie or ponderous a thing it bee, even to a thousand pounds. The Cannons and Anchors of our overwhelmed Ship were drawne up thus. I have seene that the Haven of the Ile of Male, being full of great Rocks, so that the Ships could not ride nor anchor in safetie, clensed and made navigable thus in lesse then five dayes.

Candou strange wood.

[II.ix.1655.] They use also to take five or sixe great pieces of this kind of wood, and binde them fast in a row, and above set sawed Plankes of the same Tree after the fashion of a Hurdle, after elevate it with little boords round, before, and behinde, and on the sides, and in the middle to sit. This serves them to goe to Sea, and passe from Ile to Ile: they principally fish in such, every man hath one, for they need but one to guide and conduct them. Another propertie of this Tree is, that rubbing pieces one against another, fire comes forth, and this is their kindling of fire. For chaulke they use shells found on the Sea side, which joynes and conglutinats their buildings very well together.

Fire how kindled.

They have two languages in use. The first, which is particular to the Maldives and is very ample. The second is the Arabick, which they greatly esteeme and learne as wee doe Latine. Also it serveth them daily for their holies. In the Atollon of Souadou, and toward the South of the Maldives they speake a language hard to understand, and very clounish and rude.

Languages.

They apparell themselves thus. First the men tye about their privities a great swath-band of cloth, which comes round about them, for feare that going or comming, or in doing any worke, they might be discovered. After they put a little cloth of cotton died blew, or red, or some other colour, which goes no lower then their knees. Upon that they put a great piece of cloth of cotton or silk (if they are a little rich and wealthy) which reacheth to their ankles, and gird it with a faire square handkerchiefe imbroidered with gold and silke, which they fold in three corners, and spreading it upon their backes make it fast before; after for greater ornament they adde a little piece of silke of divers colours, transparent as cobweb laune, which is short and extends no further then the middle of their thighs: and after all that they incompasse themselves in a great girdle of silke, which is like to their turbant, and is well fringed; they let the ends hang before. Within this girdle, which serves them for a purse, they put their money, and their bettele on the left side; and on the right side they weare their knife, which they

Their apparell.

Girdle.

esteeme very honourable, and there is no bodie but weares one, no not the King. These knives are very well made, all of excellent steele, for they have no invention to mingle yron with steele. They which have any meanes, weare the haft and sheath all of silver wrought and fashioned. In the end of the sheath on the top they have a buckle of silver, whereat hangs a little chaine also of silver, whereto are tyed their tooth-pickers and eare-pickers, and other little instruments. Others, which have not meanes to have them so costly, weare the sheath of wood wrought, the haft of a fishes bone, as of a Whale or other Sea creature, for they will not weare bone of any Land creature. They are very curious of their knives, and thinke themselves not well clothed, except they have them at their girdle.

Knife.

No land-bone worne.

They are not suffered to carry other Armes, except the Souldiers and Officers of the King, and they onely while they are in service of the King in the Ile of Male, or elsewhere sent by him. They have commonly at their side a waved dagger, which they call a Cris; they come from Achen, Java, and China. And moreover when they goe in the street, they alwayes carry their sword naked in one hand, and their buckler in the other, or else a javelin. Their principall braverie, is to weare about their girdle many chaines of silver. There is not one man nor woman, boy nor girle, little or great, which will not have of them according to the proportion of their goods and substance. Thereon they put their Treasure, and ordinarily designe it to defray the expences of their Funerals. But none except the Grand Lords and Strangers weare them upon their clothes to be seene: the other weare them hid underneath: and yet they will have them to speake of them, and shew privately. The residue of their bodie from the Girdle upward is naked; I understand of the common people, for the Signiors of qualitie are not so. Yet in their Feast dayes they cover themselves with Jerkins and Cassocks of Cotton or Silke which they fasten with Buttons of Gilt Copper. These Jerkins are

No Armes ordinarie.

Silver chaines.

Nakednesse.

Jerkins.

of all sorts of colours, but the edges are welted with white and blue. The sleeves come but to their elbow; they say, if they should descend to the wrist, as ours, they should not have the free mannaging of their armes. They put on also coloured linings, which are very strait, and reach from the ankles to the wast, which they fasten also on the bottome with gilded buttons.

The chiefe men array themselves ordinarily with Jerkins and Cassockes. A great number on Feast dayes use another kinde of gallantry: they bruise Sanders and Camphire on very slicke and smooth stones (which they bring from the firme Land) and sometimes other sorts of odoriferous wood; after they compound it with water distilled of flowres, and overspread their bodies with this paste, from the Girdle upwards, adding many formes with their finger, such as they imagine: it is somewhat like cut and pinked Doublets, and of an excellent savour. Sometimes they bind together faire flowres, and of the best sent. They dresse their Wives or Lemmons in this sort, and make upon their backes workes and shadowes, as they please. This is one kind of bravery which is much used, but they dare not present themselves so trimmed before the King, nor within the Palace. Upon their heads they weare red Turbants, or diversified into various colours, the richer sort of Silke, the poorer of fine Cotton. The Souldiers and Officers of the King attire themselves after one fashion, which is not permitted to others, putting often on their heads imbroydered Hand-kerchiefes, which others may not. All the people goe naked on their feet, and often on their legges, yet within their Houses they use a kind of Slippers or Sandals made of wood, but when any of their Superiours come to visit them, they pull off their Sandals, and remaine with bare feet.

Past-garment.

Skin-prints.

Souldiers and Officers attire.

Barefeet.

[II.ix.1656.]

The women have a great cloth of Cotton, or of coloured Silke which comes about them from their middle to their ankles, and serves them for a Coate. Upon that they put a Robe of Taffata, or very light Cotton, but very long: It descends to their feet, the borders are blue and

Womens habit.

white; it is very like the Smocks which women weare in these parts. It is a little open on the necke, and fastned with two little gilded Buttons, and so before in the Throate, without any more opening in the bosome: so that when they will give their children sucke, they are constrayned to pull up their Garments, yet without any indecencie, by reason of the cloth which they use in stead
Bracelets heavie. of a Coate. Their Armes are laden with great Bracelets of Silver, sometimes from the wrist to the elbow; the poorer sort weare them mixed with Brasse, others of fine and massie Silver, so that there are some found with three or foure pound of Silver on their Armes: and moreover they have Chaines of Silver on their Girdles under their clothes, which are not seene, but sometimes when their
Chaines. Garments are very lightsome. They have many Chaines of Gold about their neckes if they be women of ranke and fashion, or they knit together pieces of Gold Coine, which comes thither from Arabia, or elsewhere from the Continent. In their eares they weare very rich pendants according to their wealth, but they weare them not after the same fashion we doe heere. For the Mothers pierce the eares of their Daughters when they are young, not only in the lap or fat of the eare, but all along the gristle
Eare-tires. in many places, and put there threeds of Cotton to encrease and keepe the holes, that they may put when they are greater little gilded nailes, to the number of twentie foure in both eares. The head of the naile is commonly adorned with a precious Stone or Pearle, also in the lap of the eare they have an earing fashioned after their manner. When the women goe in the streets either in the night or day, (although they go seldome in the day) they weare a Veile upon their heads; but they put it downe going with the Queenes or great Ladies, or with their betters, but not at all before men, no, not before the King; but on the contrary they will hide themselves more when they imagine that men eye them.

It is observable, that none neither man nor woman, except the Prince or Grand Signior dare weare any Rings set with Stones, nor Jewels, nor Bracelets, Carkanets, or Earings, nor Chaines of Gold without permission from the King, if they bee men, or from the Queenes, if they bee women. This permission they buy, except they conferre this benefit on them, as they doe often to the women.

None, neither Queenes nor Princesses may weare Bracelets and Rings of Gold on their Armes and Legs: but for any other ornament it is permitted them to have Gold; but although the Rings of their Feet and Legges are of Silver, they may not weare what quantitie they will, if they be not of great Birth and Originall, nor put Rings on their fore-fingers, except the Queenes, the Princesses and great Ladies on the middle-fingers; all other women with permission on the two other fingers, the men only on their thumbe. So every one knowes his ranke and degree, and what ornaments he must have aswell for himselfe as his Wife, and there is no confusion in it, If the Wife of any one which hath not accustomed to goe brave before, beginne to goe more gay, or if a man weare Rings set with Jewels on his finger, although in so doing hee exceeds not that which is permitted him; yet they impose on him a greater Taxe for this: except the Officers of the King and of the Queenes, which pay no Taxes, nor the Inhabitants of the Ile of Malé, yet they are burthened with other charges, and pay many extraordinary expences. The Strangers and their Wives have priviledge to attire themselves as they wil, to weare what ornaments and costlinesse they will, without permission, even as the great Princes, or the King himselfe. In briefe I observed, that the Strangers have more Priviledges and Immunities then the Naturals. Also the Pandiare, the Naybes and Catibes of the Ile of Malé, and other Ilands may dresse and array themselves as they please, without being bound to the Lawes for this thing as others.

Gold prohibited.

Strangers priviledged.

The women are curious to tricke and trimme themselves handsomely. They have a custome to make the nailes of their feet and hands red. This is the beautie of

Womens customes.

the Countrey: they make it with the juice and moysture of a certayne Tree, and it endures as long as their nailes. Certainly they appeare very faire and beautifull, aswell because they attire themselves neatly, as because they are wel-favoured, of a good proportion, and very prettie.

[II.ix.1657.]

§. IIII.

Rites of Meate and Drinke, Bathing, Superstitious Observations: Diseases. Education of Children. Fishing, Fashions, Lusts.

Feasting. THey never eate together, but with men of their owne Ranke and Qualitie; counting it a dishonour to eate with their inferiour: Also they feast seldome, except at their Festivals and Solemnities. If they wil at other times entertaine their friends, they prepare a Service of many Dishes, and set it on a great round Table covered with Taffata, and send it into his House whom they will feast: which they hold a great honour. *Feeding.* Being in their owne house they love not the others should see them eate, and goe therefore to the furthest side of their house, letting downe all the clothes and Tapistrie which are before them, that so they may be unseene. Before they eate, they say their Prayers. They have no other Table then the floore of their Lodgings, which is covered with a little fine Mat, whereon they sit crosse-legged. *Neatnesse.* They use no Naperie, but for feare of wasting their Mats they use great leaves of the Bannanes whereon they set their Dishes, and others before them in stead of Trenchers: they are so neat in their feeding, that they shed nothing in the place where they eate, no not one drop of water, although they wash their mouth before and after their repast. *Dishes.* Their dishes are of Earth, figured after the maner of the Country, and come from Cambaya; as good as China Porcelane, and so common that all use them. But they have no Platter of Earth or Porcelane, which is not after the fashion of a Box round, varnished and nealed, and a cover of the same matter. The poorer sort have covered Platters in stead of these Boxes, which cost little. The reason is because of the Ants, which in great numbers fill every place, so that it is very difficult to keepe any thing without a cover. *Pismires troublesome.*

They are also so nice in their Diet, that they will not taste of any meate wherein hath fallen a Flye or an Emit, or any little creature, or the least filthinesse, so that they will give it to the Birds when they come: for they have no minde to give it to the poore, to whom they never give any thing which they would not have, or which is not aswell dressed as for themselves. Wherefore when the poore come to their doores, they make them come in, and make them as good cheere as for themselves; saying, that they are the Servants of God aswell as themselves. The Grand Signiors and rich men have no other Vessels then other men, although they might have them of Gold and Silver, yet their Law forbids it. If a dish happen to be a little riven or crackt, they eate no more in it; saying, that it is polluted. They use no Spoones neither to eate Rice nor Honey, nor any liquid thing, but take them with their fingers, which they doe neatly and nimbly without losing any thing, for they account it the greatest incivilitie in the World to let any thing fall in eating. In the meane while also, none dare spit nor cough, but must rise and goe forth. In eating they never use the left hand, because therewith they wash their Privities. They willingly eate at the beginning of their feeding a Cocos halfe ripe, and drinke the water of it; saying, that it is healthfull, and looseth their belly. They eate all greedily and in haste, holding it mannerlinesse not to be long in eating: and in the meane while, though they be in company, they speake not a word. *Nicetie.* *Charitie.* *No Plate.* *Finger-spoons.* *Dexteritie.* *Quicke at meate.*

To drinke while they are eating, is reckond clownishnesse, but after they have eaten their fill, they drinke once. Their drinke is commonly of water, or of Wine of Cocos drawne forth the same day: they have also other sorts of drinkes for the King and Nobles, or at their great Solemnities. They drinke in Copper Cups well wrought, *Drinking rites.*

Bettell. with covers on them. After their repast, and when they have washed, they present a Platter of Bettell, in stead of sweet meates. For the most part they have no ordinarie houre of eating, but eate at all houres when they are hungry. Their Wives and Daughters prepare and dresse their meate, and not men. It is the greatest injurie that a man can doe to one, to call him Cisday, that is to say Cooke: and if any bee found to addict themselves to this, they are mocked and despised every where, in such sort that they esteeme them not for men but women: and they dare not accompany with any but women, nor doe any other exercise; also they make it no difficultie to leave them with them.

No man cooke.

Butcher-rites. When they kill any creature for their food, they have many Mysteries. They cut the throat turning themselves toward Mahomets Sepulchre, and say their Prayers, and all speedily let it goe, or goe forth, not touching it till it be thoroughly dead. If any touch it before, they cast away the flesh, and eate it not. Also they cut it not every-where, but in a certaine place of the throat, otherwise they eat it not, and every one understands not this, but principally their Priests or Mondius know it: they which enterprize it must bee ancient and not yong, and such as have had children. In all their actions they are very scrupulous and superstitious. After they have slept, whether in the night or day, they faile not presently after they are awake, to wash their eyes and face, and rub them with Oyle, and put also a certaine blacknesse upon their eye-lids and eye-browes: they dare not speake nor bid any good morrow till they have done thus; they are carefull to rub their Teeth, and to wash and clense them, saying furthermore, that the Red colour of Bettell and Arecka, which they chawe continually takes the better: so that they have all red Teeth, by reason of champing of Bettell, & they account this braverie. They carrie it also alwaies about in the pleats of their Girdle, and it should be a dishonor to be found without it; it is the custome when they encounter one another by the way interchange-

Superstition.

[II.ix.1658.]

Bettell and Arecka.

ably each to give the other some of his. They bathe often in the day, not only for pleasure and commoditie, but for Religion, or entrance into the Mosche: they wash their Extreems after they have made urine, or done their necessities, they wash their Privities with the left hand, or they wash all their bodie, which they call Junan, according to their Feasts with diversities of formes and ceremonies. So that when they wash in publike, as they doe, a man may know wherefore they bathe, as if they have accompanied with their Wives whether by night or by day, they plunge their head three times under the water. When they are to goe any Voyage, they desire not to meet or touch any body, and if any disastrous thing chance to them, they attribute it to him who toucht them. Above al when they goe on fishing, they must not salute any, nor bid them good morrow. From the going downe of the Sunne on Thursday in the Evening, till the day following about three or foure of the clocke, they will not permit any thing to be carried out of their Houses, although their deerest Love, or their Father would borrow any thing, they would not give it them, neither will they render that which shall be sent for, although it bee not theirs: yet they will receive any thing, and let it enter into their houses in the meane-while without any scruple. They wrangle not nor quarrell together, although there be enmitie betweene them; above all take heed of reproaching.

Bathing.

Superstitions.

In sailing, if they be surprized with contrarie winds, of calmes, or stormes, they make Vowes to him which commands the winds, whom they call not God, but King. There is no Ile where is not found a Siare, as they call it, which is a place dedicated to the winds, in a desolate corner of the Ile, where they which have escaped danger, make Offerings daily of little Boates and ships made purposely, full of Perfumes, Gummes, Flowres, and odoriferous Woods. They burne the Perfumes, and cast the little Boats into the Sea which goe floting till they be burned, for they put fire in them; to the end, they say,

Their Æolus-rites.

that the King of the Winds may accept them. Also they set not willingly their ships and Gallies afloate, but they kill Hens and Cockes, and cast them in the Sea before the ship or Boat which they will use. They beleeve also that there is a King of the Sea, to whom in like sort they make Praiers and Ceremonies in their Navigation, and when they goe on fishing, fearing upon everie errour and offence, the Kings of the Winds and of the Sea. So that being on the Sea they dare not spit on the windie side, nor cast any thing overboord, for feare that they should be angrie with them: also they never looke behind them. All the Boates, Barkes, and ships are devoted to the powers of the Winds and of the Sea: and surely they respect them as if they were their Temple, keeping them neate, and never committing any filthy and dishonest thing in them. They have also the Kings of the other Elements (as they call them) and especially that of Warre, but all with great Ceremonies.

Superstitious neatnesse.

Characters. See the like in Jobsons Notes of Gambra.

They greatly esteeme certaine Characters, which they call Tavide, which they weare under their Garments, inclosed in little Boxes, which the Rich make of Gold or Silver. They weare them often on their armes, on their necke, or at their Girdle, or else at their foot, according to the subject of the Disease; for they weare them for all things as well offensive as defensive, that they should love or be loved, or hate, or to heale or cure any Maladie. The Magicians and Sorcerers sell them these for monie, and tell them that it brings them good lucke, and heales their Diseases. They have few remedies for their Maladies, but have recourse to the Magicians and Sorcerers, who are their only Physicians. They beleeve also that all their evill is caused by the Devill to vexe them, who is the only cause of their Deaths and Diseases. Therefore they call upon him, and offer Flowres to him, and prepare Banquets of all sorts of Viands and Beverages, which they set in a certaine secret place, where they let them consume, if no poore people happen to take them away. For the same purpose they kill Cockes or Hennes, turning

Magicians.

Devil invoked.

them towards the Sepulchre of Mahomet, after leaving them there, praying the Devill to accept of them.

The Fever is common among them, but most dangerous to strangers. From ten yeeres to ten yeeres, here comes a Disease called Curivadiri, for which they abandon one another, as if it were the Plague. It is like the small Pockes, and kils many. The diseases of the Eyes are very common, I have seene a great number blind, and the most part have little Eyes. It happens also often that having beene long in the Sunne in the height of the day, after the Sunne is downe, they see not at all, whatsoever fire or light be put neere them, although it were a hundred Torches, yet without feeling any other evill. To heale it, they boyle the Liver of a Cocke, and write words and Charmes, and set it toward the point of the setting of the Sunne. My Companions and I were sometimes vexed with this Maladie: but having learned the Receit, wee tooke the Liver of a Cocke, rejecting their Charmes, to see if that would serve, and wee found that it healed us as well as them, without observing their Sorceries. They are much subject to the Itch, which they heale with Oyle of Cocos. Remedilesse Tetters terrifie them much: some have almost their whole bodies over-runne with them. These evils come by reason of the quantitie of Salt-fish which they eate, and also because they seldome salt their meates, but powre Sea-water to it.

Fevers. *Decenniall Disease.* *Blindnesse.* *Tetters.* [II.ix.1659.]

In the Winter, although the Raines are continuall, yet they goe bare-foot, they have under their feet and betweene their toes, a kind of hand-worme, which breeds in the filth, it maketh Wheales and Pushes full of water, which after they increase ingender Ulcers, which greatly hinders their going. They are also troubled all over the bodie with these Wormes. They have all commonly great Spleenes, and are subject to obstructions, and endure much evill. They have some Receits and Compositions of Herbes and Drugges for divers Maladies, and principally for wounds, which they heale very cunningly.

Bare-foot. *Feet wormes.* *Splenetike.*

They use no bindings nor linnen to their Soares, but

Rheumes. only Ointments. Cathaires and Fluxes sometimes trouble them, and aches in the bones. The Neapolitan disease is not very frequent: they heale it with China wood, without sweating or any other thing, they call it Farangui Baesrour, this Maladie came from Europe, whose Inhabitants they call Farangui or Frangui. They are never troubled with the Tooth-ache; it seemes their ordinary chawing of Bettell is the cause hereof. As soone as their Infants are borne, they wash them in cold water sixe times a day, and after they chafe them with Oyle, and continue this washing a great while: and moreover, when they make Urine, or doe Natures Office, they wash their Privities with water.

Europeans called Frankes.

No Toothache.

Hardinesse.

Nurserie of Infants. The Mothers nourish their owne Children, and dare not put them forth to nurse to others, no not the Queenes, saying ordinarily that the beasts bring up their young, but they have Servants to tend, carrie, and governe them. Besides the breast they make a kind of Pappe, of Rice or Honey, brayed and macerated, after boiled with Milke and Sugar of Cocos. The most part (especially the poorest) give them Bananes. They never swaddle their Children, but let them goe free, and yet I never saw any deformed. Now their Couch hangs in the Aire, within little Beds of coard, or little Chaires, where they shogge and rocke them. At the age of nine moneths they begin to goe.

Education. At nine yeeres old they bring them up in the studies and exercises of the Countrey. These studies are to learne to write and to reade, and to understand their Alcoran, and know what they are bound to doe. Their Letters are of divers sorts, the Arabicke with some Letters and Points which they have added to expresse their Language: another whereof the Character is peculiar to the Language of the Maldives, and moreover, a third which is the vulgar of Ceylan, and of the greatest part of the Indies. They write their Lessons on little Tables of wood, which are white, and when they can say their Lesson by heart, they blot it out, and white it againe. If the writing bee to abide and remaine perpetually, they write upon Parchment

Letters peculiar.

Learning to write.

which is made of the leafe of the Tree called Macore Queau, which is a fathome and an halfe in length, and a foot broad. To teach their Children to write, they have Boards made of wood purposely, very smooth and plaine, whereon they spread very fine and thinne Sand, after with a Bodkin they make the Letters, and make them imitate them, blotting out the Rule which they have written, and never use herein any Paper. *Leafe Parchment.*

They carrie as great respect and reverence to their Tutors as to their Fathers: so that they may not contract Marriage together, as being allied in Affinitie. There are some found among them who follow their studies, who are very skilfull in the Alcoran, and Ceremonies of their Law; they are principally the Modins, Catibes, or Naybes. These two Offices are compatible, for a Catibe may be a Naybe, and a Naybe a Catibe. *New Kindred of Teachers.*

The Mathematickes are there taught, and are greatly esteemed, especially Astrologie, which many studie; for they consult with the Astrologers about every thing: They will enterprize nothing without their advice. They will not only know their Nativities and time of their Births, but also if they build, whether with wood or stone, they must enquire of the Astrologer, what houre will bee best to beginne, that it may bee under a good Constellation: or if they employ a Boate, although they doe it diversly, taking a different day or houre for a ship of Warre, or of Merchandize, or a fishing Barke. If they undertake any Voyage, or any thing else, they enquire of the Astrologer what shall be the issue, and whether the day bee good or evill, if the Planet be favourable or unfortunate. Whatsoever sinister accident happens to them, they attribute the cause to the day, and take it patiently, saying, it is the will of God that hath brought it to passe. *Astrologie.* *Divinations.*

The Ilanders are much exercised in Armes, either to serve with a Sword and Buckler, or readily to bend the Bow, or use the Harquebuse, or mannage the Pike: they have Schooles, the Masters whereof are greatly honoured and respected, and ordinarily the Grand Signiors use this *Armes.*

exercise. They have no plaies but the Ball and Tennice, which they receive and cast forth with great agilitie, although it be not but with their feet.

Fishing. Their greatest exercise is fishing, which all in all places of the Maldives use indifferently, without having any (as in other places) certaine persons of this vocation, or certaine places proper to it, which are not publike. This exercise they account honest and honorable wherein also the Gentlemen exercise themselves as they doe heere in hunting. The King hath twelve persons appointed to guide and conduct his Boat when he goeth on fishing, and to prepare all things necessarie for it.

[II.ix.1660.] They have an admirable quantitie of great Fish, as Bonitos, Albachores, guilt-heads and others which are very like one another, and of the same taste, and have no more skales then the Mackrell. They take them in the deepe Sea, on this fashion, with a line of a fathom and a halfe of great round Cotton thred made fast to a great Cane. Their hooke, is not so much bowed as ours, but more stretched out, & is pointed in the end like a Pin, without having any other beard or tongue. They fasten not on their Bait, but the day before provide a quantitie of small Fish, as great as our little Bleaks, or Roches, which they find in great number on the Bankes and Sands, and keep them alive inclosed in little pursnets (made of the Thred of Cocos) with little Mashes, and let them hang in the Sea at the Sterne of their Barkes. When they come into the deepe Sea, they sow about their little Fishes, and let their Line hang downe. The great Fish seeing the little Fish, which is not frequent in the deepe Sea, runne together in great shoales, and by the same meanes they fastem them to their hookes, which they white and trim over; so that being a ravenous and foolish Fish, it takes the whited Hook, thinking it is a white little Fish. They doe nothing but lift their Line into their Boat, and the Fish falls off presently (being not strongly fastened) and then they put it into the Sea againe; thus they take a strange quantitie, so that in three or foure houres their Boates are in a

Strange formes of taking fish.

manner full; and that which is remarkable, they go alwayes with full sayle. The Fish which they take thus they generally cal in their language Cobolly Masse, that is to say, the Blacke Fish, for they are all blacke.

They have another sort of fishing on their bankes, when the Moone is in the change, and when it is at the full, three daies each time. This they doe on Rafts made of the Wood, called Camdou. They have great Lines of fiftie or sixtie fathome pitched over. In the end they hang hookes wheron they fasten the baite as we doe, and thus take great quantitie of fish, one kinde very delicious, which they call the King of the Sea. They have all sorts of Nets and Toiles made of Cotton twine, Weeles and other Instruments of fishing. Neere the Sea shoare, and where it is shallow, they passe their time, and take delight in fishing for small fish, like Pilchards with casting Nets. Twice in the Yeere at the Equinoctials, they make a generall fishing, a great number of persons assemble together in certaine indraughts of the Sea. The Sea at that time ariseth higher then all the times of the Yeere, and passeth the limits of other Tides, the Ebbe after the same proportion recoiles and retires, discovering the Rockes and Shoalds, which at other times appeare not. In these places while the Sea is going out, they observe some fit corner, and set about it great stones, one upon another to a great height, so that it resembles a round Wall or Raveling. This inclosure hath fortie paces in circuit or compasse: but the entrance is but two or three paces large. They gather together thirtie or fortie men, and every one carrieth fiftie or sixie fathome of great coard of Cocos, where from fathome to fathome they tie a piece of the Barke of dried Cocos, to make it float on the water, as we use Corke: after, they tye them together, and stretch them out in a round upon the flats. It is strange, that all the fish which is within the coard, finding themselves taken, although there bee no other Nets nor Instruments, but the Coard which swimmeth on the water, but the fish fearing the Line and shadow of the Line; so that they dare not passe

King of the Sea.

Generall fishing.

under to escape, but flye from the Line, thinking that it hath a Net underneath: The men goe all driving them to the inclosure of stone, drawing up the coard by little and little some in Boates, and some in the water (for upon these flats the Sea is shallow, and not above necke high for the most part lesse) so moderately drawing up the Line, the fish flye from it, and are locked up in the inclosure, so that in the end the Line being all drawne up, all the fishes enter in: and they speedily stop the entry with Faggots of boughes and leaves of Cocos, bound end to end, twentie or thirtie fathome, and compacted together about the greatnesse of a man, and so when the Sea is out, the fish remaine taken on the dry Land. They often take thus of all sorts ten and twelve thousand or more. This fishing they make but once in sixe monethes, upon every flat, and every time continues five daies, and they change daily their divisions, and returne not often into the same place to fish in this manner, except at another Equinoctiall.

The people are above measure superstitious, and addicted to their Religion: but yet extreamly given to women, wanton and riotous. There is nothing commoner then Adulteries, Incest and Sodomie, notwithstanding the rigour of their Lawes and Penalties: As for simple Fornication, there is nothing more ordinarie: they count it not a sinne, neither their Wives, nor Daughters which are not married, make it no great matter to yeeld themselves to their Friends, and after (which is very execrable) to evacuate their Fruit by making an abortion, or destroy *Lecherie.* their children which are not legitimate. The women are strangely impudent, and the men are not lesse vitious (but they cannot be more) and very effeminate. All their desire is to procure (if they can) some Receit, that they may better content their Wives, and be more strong to exercise their Fornications. I thinke they spend all their goods on this; hereof they continually speake, and are very dissolute in their words, and almost never stirre from their Wives, of whom they have pluralitie, to three, which is the cause that they cannot satisfie each of them: also the

Aire of the Countrey is hot, and exhales part of their spirits and courage: and also their continually softening their flesh in the water, and that the most part eate Opium, or Aphion, as they call it, which tipples, intoxicates and [II.ix.1661.] duls them. The women (as I have said) carefully hide their brests: to speake of them, they account very lascivious and dishonest. To kisse, they make as great a matter as to lye together, although they be dissolute in their conversation, yet they containe themselves before their Parents, and respect their presence. But if a man happen to speake a word (such as I have said) to a woman before one or any of her Kindred, they will goe hide themselves, and be greatly offended against him; he must therefore make them excuses, and say that hee knew not that they were neere of kin; otherwise they will thinke that he did purposely, and therefore complaine to the Justice, that hee may manifest which said these lascivious words in their presence, that he holds them for good and honest people. A man dare not enter into the place where a woman bathes her selfe, or where she is retired (her Robe being off) although they never take off the cloth which environs them, and serves them for a Coat; but (as I have said) they esteeme the brests as shamefull parts.

Breasts not to be spoken of.

When a man and woman is together, and another person meet with him, hee must not demand of this man if she be his Wife, or Daughter, or Sister: for if it were his Daughter, and hee should aske if it were his Wife, he should offend as if he accused him of Incest; only he must demand if she be his Kinswoman, & he tels the degree of Parentage or Affinitie. As long as the woman have their tearmes, they bathe not, and wash only their hands and mouth, they change not their Garments, nor lie with their Husbands, nor eate nor converse with any bodie. When the women goe a visiting in the night, they must have a man to accompany them who goeth before, and when hee perceives that any body comes, hee saith three times Gas, that is, take heede: the men advertised

Visitation.

by this, quite the side of the way where the woman goes, making no semblance of seeing them, nor of knowing them, with great respect: and if they bee other women, they take each her side of the way, and salute not, except they bee very familiar. They never knocke at the Gate (for there is no Ring or Hammer) nor call to bee let into the house, for the great Gate of the Court is alwayes open till eleven of the clocke in the evening: wherefore they enter into the Court, which is neere the doore of the house, which is also open and spread onely with Tapestrie of Cotton cloth, or other stuffe, and as they approach to this Gate, they cough once, which they hearing within, go forth and see if any one would speake with them. Also the men going in the night through the street, cough often determinately, that they may advertise one the other, for feare of hurting, or wounding, for they carry their weapons naked; I understand the Souldiers and Officers of the King in the Ile of Male.

§. V.

Their Government described. The Judges, Officers, Gentry, Communaltie. The King his Palace, Guard, Nobilitie, Robes, Attire, Attendance, Exercises, Riches; slaine by the Bengalans.

The King. THe government of the estate of the Maldives is royall and very absolute and ancient; the King is feared and reverenced, and all depend of him. In each of the thirteene Cantons is one principall, whom they call Naybe. *Naybe.* These Naybes or principalls of the Provinces are Priests and Doctors of their Law, and have the oversight of all that concernes Religion, and instruction of the people therein, and exercise of Justice, and command the Priests which are under them. These Atollons are subdivided into many Ilands, in each of which, where there is not above fortie and one men, is a Doctor called Catibe, *Catibe.* superior in the Religion of that Ile, who hath under him the particular Priests of the Moschees, all which have care to nourish and instruct the people in the Law; and live of a certaine portion of fruits which every one is bound to give them, and of certaine rents which the King gives them according to their degree. But particularly the Naybes, besides the exercise of Religion, and authoritie which they have, are instituted to execute and doe justice, each in his government. They are the onely Judges of the Country as well in matters civill as criminall, and if any one will have justice hee must goe finde out the Naybe, or attend his comming to the place. For the Naybes foure times in the yeere, go in circuit about the Ilands, each in his Jurisdiction, and make Visitations, as wel for the religion of the Priests, as for justice. This is their greatest revenue, for then their duties are paid them: moreover they receive store of Presents from many persons, whereof they are very greedie. In all the Maldives there are no Judges but the thirteene Naybes; for the Catibes of the Ilands, and the Priests of the Moschees are but for a shew.

Their maintenance.

The thirteene Naybes. Visitation and Circuit.

Over these Naybes there is a superior, which resides in the Ile of Male (and is ever neere his person) which is called Pandiare; who is not onely chiefe of the Religion throughout all the Realme, but also soveraigne Judge. So that after they have pleaded before the Naybe, if they will not stand to his sentence, whether in matters civill or criminall, they may appeale to the Pandiare: who discides all affaires that offer themselves, taking advise of some Naybes which are neere him, of the Catibes, grave men called Moucouris, that is Doctors and experienced men, which are not Officers: they give no judgement if they be not assisted with foure or five of these persons at the least. These Moucouries can say all the Alcoran by heart (and all the others read it onely) besides divers other Sciences which they know. They solemnely invite them to all their Feasts, Sermons, and Ceremonies; and are greatly honoured and respected by all. There are not above fifteene of them in all the Ilands. The Pandiare is called Cady in the Arabick language.

The Pandiare or chiefe Judge.

[II.ix.1662.]

Moucouries learned men.

The King. *Sixe Councellours of State.* Also after the judgement of the Pandiare, one may complaine to the King, who commands, and makes justice to be executed: and this is by six Signiors his principall Officers, who manage the most importune affaires of state. The Pandiare being assisted with two Catibes of the Ile of Malé, and by Naybe of the Attollon, besides some of those Doctors, goeth also to make his visitation through the Ile of Malé, as every Naybe in his Atollon; and hee is attended with his Officers which carry a long whip to correct delinquents. Hee makes all (without exception) that meet him, to say their creed, and some prayers in the Arabick tongue, and after demands the interpretation in *Severe Catechising.* the Maldive language; and if they are ignorant, he causeth them to be whipt and scourged in the open field by his Officers. The women dare not shew themselves when hee goeth through the street, and if hee encounter any unvailed, hee causeth her haire to be shaven.

Treasurer. Besides the Naybes, there is in every Atollon a man delegated and appointed by the King to receive and levie his rents and revenues. All the Iles have each their order by Division and Cantons, as that of Malé; there are five divisions which they call Avares, and each hath a principall *Avares.* called Mouscouly Avare: the ancient of the division, and nothing is done there for the King or the people, but they come to him. Justice (which they call in their language Sacouest) is exercised in the house of the Naybe, or else in the Ile of Malé in the house of the Pandiare, and sometimes in the Kings Palace when the matter is of weight or moment. When they will begin a suit, they goe to the *Sergeants.* Judge or Naybe, who sends one of the Sergeants (of whom there are a certaine number, called Devanits) to make the accused partie come; and if he bee in the same Iland, hee must have to make him come, a letter of the Naybe, by the meanes whereof he must notifie the place where he is, seeing that he is in the Jurisdiction of the Naybe. Or else if hee be of another Jurisdiction, the Naybe can doe *Writs.* nothing, but in this case he must have letters of the Pandiare, who can make him come from any part of the

Realme into the Kings Iland, where he abideth. Now they give this letter to the Catibe, superior of the Ile, who in presence of them all gives it to the partie accused, expresly charging him to goe thither: hereof they dare not faile, for they which disobey this justice, cannot associate with any, nor goe to the Mosche, nor eate nor drinke with them, and they hold them not of their Law. If it bee so that any will not obey, or if hee be some Grande, the King sends his Souldiers to constraine him to come. But if hee will not plead before the Naybe, either because hee beares him ill will, or because that his partie hath too much favour against him, then the plaintiffe or the defendant who is accused, goeth to find out the King, who commands that hee doe Justice by Judges not suspected. This they execute in the Kings house, in the presence of all the chiefe of the Iland. The parties plead their owne causes themselves. If the cause bee of fact, each bring three witnesses, and if they have them not, the defendant is beleeved on his oath only, which they take in touching with the hand the book of their law, which the Judge presents; and then the plaintiffe if hee bee a little versed in affaires, markes scrupulously if the party touched the booke really, and the place where he did it. If the difference bee in matter of right, they are judged by the Law.

Excommunication.

No Advocates.

Cases de facto & de jure.

The Judges take nothing for their judgements, for nothing is due, except that the Devonits or Sergeants have the twelfth part of that which is due or adjudged. The Slaves cannot bee witnesses, nor plead, nor make triall in judgement; likewise in such a cause they receive three women for one man. The Slaves are such as make themselves so, or such as they bring from other places and sell; for shipwrackt strangers lose not the libertie which they had; if they were Slaves they remaine so. The Slaves which they call Allo, are of worst conditions. They can have but one wife although all others have three. Beating of a Slave is punished with halfe that which they inflict for beating a Free-man. Debtors are constrained, if they have nothing to pay, to yeeld themselves Servants and not

Slaves.

Debtors.

Slaves, and are not used as such, but as naturalls of the Countrie, and serve onely their Creditors or other persons which lend them mony to discharge them, these are called Pemousere, which is to say, servant by borrowing, and they continue thus till they are acquitted, yea their children are Slaves perpetually if they pay it not. Yet when they are ill intreated, they may discharge them, ingaging themselves in the same sort to another, that lends it them: for all their service they are nourished and maintained, and when they die their Masters takes all that they had, and if there be not enough to satisfie him, the children must serve till hee bee paid. There are many which seeke (to bee these Pemoussere) to great persons and men of authoritie, to have support and favour: for when they belong to no body, they are troubled by one or other.

Children. The wife cannot pursue in justice the death of her husband: but onely the children or the kindred. If the children be young, they stay till they be sixteene yeeres old, to know if they will revenge the death of their father. While they thus stay, the Judge commands him which is [II.ix.1663.] appeached of murther to bring up the children of the deceased, and teach them some Trade or Mysterie. When they are come to age, they demand Justice, or remit and pardon the Murtherer, without any after examination. In matters of injury committed on the person of any particular, the wronged must complaine; or otherwise the crime is abolished: except the King will make justice to be executed, without the other partie, but this is seldome.

Punishments. The ordinary punishments are banishment into the desart Ilands towards the South; cutting off a principall member; or the whip, which is the commonest punishment, but extraordinarily cruell. *Terrible whips.* They are thongs of great thicke leather, a fathom in length, foure fingers in breadth, and two in thicknesse: hereof there are five or sixe tied together, in a stocke and handle of Wood. With this they chastice malefactors, and beat them so severely that they die often. This is the ordinary punishment (for the most part) of the greatest crimes, as Sodomy, Incest, and Adultery. Besides this punishment, they cut off the womens hayre that are taken in adultery. False witnesses, and perjured persons are thus punished, and moreover condemned in a pecuniary mulct, which is disposed of to the poore. A rape is punished as adultery, and (for the most part) the ravisher is condemned to endow the woman or mayd. The stealing of any thing of valew, with the cutting off the hand. If they commit any thing against the Law, they must make a kinde of publike penance. They thinke they shall never come in Paradice if they pay not, and accomplish that which the Law hath appointed. For the execution and chastising of malefactors, they have no hangmen, but the Devanits or Sergeants doe it. For punishment with death, although their Law ordaines it for Homicide, yet the Judges never condemne them to it. All the while I was in the Maldives I saw none condemned to death by the ordinary Judges: they dare not doe it, except the King expresly commands it, which is seldome. They say commonly, that they must not put men to death so; and if they should execute all that merit death, it would bee a long time before the Ilands should bee inhabited. Yet the King sends his Souldiers, and condemnes and executes those as have deserved it. For although justice be in the power of the Doctors of the Law, yet the King is the onely arbitrator, and alone hath power of life and death. Among others the King useth one particular punishment on those which have offended him; hee maketh them lye on the ground upon their belly, and their armes and legges to bee held by foure men, and after to be beaten on their backe, with a staffe or kinde of cane, called Rotan, which comes from Bengala; this pulls off the skin, and the marke or brand endures perpetually.

Adultery. *Rape.* *Theft.* *Few executed.*

They never put in writing their suits and differences, nor their accusations, nor depositions, nor judgements, for they are all very readie and compendious: neither in

No writings for evidence.

civill matters, except it be about grounds of inheritance, or Cocos trees which are immoveable, and that the Pandiare or Naybes give judgement. For in this case, they give their letters sealed with their seale of Inke, for I never saw them use any Waxe, and this serves for a testimony to their offspring, that hereafter, neither hee which hath obtained the cause, nor his heyres may be disquieted.

Degrees and sorts of men. Rites, & rights of Nobilitie.

There are foure sorts of persons: in the first is comprehended the King called Rasquan, and the Queene called Renequillague, with those which are of their race, and precedent King, Princes, called Calans, Princesses or Camenaz, and Grand Signiors. The second order is that of Dignities, Offices, and Degrees, which the King distributes, wherein likewise the rankes is very carefully observed. The third is the Gentrie. The fourth, the common People. I will begin at the third, which is the ranke which birth gives to every one separate from the common people. There are many Noble men dispersed heere and there among the Iles. They which are not Nobles dare not sit with them, nor in their presence, although it bee at the further end, and as farre as they see a greater then they comming behind, they must attend and let him goe before. If also they have any piece of cloath upon their shoulder, or any thing, they put it downe. The Noble women, although they marrie with men of inferiour condition and not Noble, loose not their ranke. Yea the Children which issue from them are Noble, by reason of the Mother. Also the women of low estate marrying to Noble men, are not ennobled by their Husbands, but retayne their first ranke. Besides the Nobles by birth, the King ennobles whom hee will. Then when this happens, the King besides his Letters wherewith hee priviledgeth him, sends one of his Officers appointed for this, who makes publication throughout all the Ile, or sounds a kinde of Bell which is of cast mettall, whereon hee strikes with a Hammer. After the King, are the Princes of the bloud, and they which are descended of other Kings his predecessours, who although they be of divers Houses, yet are all much honoured and respected.

Kings Lieutenant and other Officers.

Next are the great Officers of the Kingdome: that is to say, the Quilague, which wee may call the Kings Lieutenant generall: because next to the King and in his absence, hee is most mightie in the Government of the State, so that nothing is done without his advise. Also if the King will have any thing observed or executed, hee is the first whom the King deputes, and to whom hee addresseth his commands. Next him, another called Parenas which is of great authoritie: An Endequery, whose Office is to bee alwayes neere the King, and to counsell him in all his occasions and affaires. Another hath charge of Sea matters, which wee may tearme Admirall, hee is called Velannas, hee lookes to the Ships which arrive, and their Merchandize; and hath care of entertaining Strangers and soliciting for them, hee useth to come to the ships which arrive, even the smallest Barkes, [II.ix.1664.] although they bee of the Countrey, and takes away the rudder, and causeth it to bee carried into the Kings house, for feare they should goe away without taking leave. He hath under him two Sergeants which looke to the Ships that arrive, and make him account, and obey his behests. There is a Generall over the Souldiers, called Dorimenaz, who hath also a Lieutenant, called Acouraz. Moreover there is a Chanceller, called Manpas, who sets to all letters the Kings seale, which is nothing else but his name in Arabick, ingraven in Silver, which hee dips in Inke and imprints on the paper. The Secretarie is called Carans, the Controller of the Exchequer Musbandery, and the Treasurer Ransbandery: with divers other lesser Officers. All these Grandes abovenamed are often called to give the King counsell when he pleaseth, with sixe ancient and experienced men, called Mouscoulis. Besides the rents and revenues of certaine Ilands given to these Officers, the King gives them Rice for their provision, as also to the Souldiers, with Tributes and Tolls of Barkes and Ships which come to trafficke in the Maldives. All the honour in this Countrie is to eate of the Kings Rice, and be of the number of his Officers: without this a man is not esteemed noble, although he be.

Souldiers and Gentlemen.

Next to the Officers the Souldiers are most esteemed and priviledged, and they make little account of a Gentleman if hee bee not inrolled in the Souldierie. The Souldierie consists of Souldiers of the Kings Guard which are six hundred, divided into sixe companies, commanded by the Mouscoulis. There are ten other great Companies gathered together, each whereof hath a Captayne of the Grand Signiors of the Realme. These guard not, but serve the King, when hee hath any affaires, not onely as Souldiers to march and fight, but to doe all that hee commands, as to lanch a Ship, to draw it on dry land, or to doe such great worke where there is neede of men to build his Palace, if it bee needfull, or to make any worke or edifice for him. They call them and gather them together with the sound of a certayne Bell. They divide them into parts, for there are five Companies which are more honourable, wherein they admit none but Gentlemen, and other five Companies meaner, of all sorts of persons.

None can bee entred into the Companies, before they have permission of the King, and moreover it costs him for his entrance sixtie Larins, twentie to the King for his permission, and fortie to distribute to the Companie whereof hee ought to bee. The Slaves therefore cannot bee inrolled, nor they which get their living and substance from the Coco Trees, nor any mechanicall and base people, and generally those which cannot write and reade, nor those which serve others. Moreover they buy for the most part all Offices of the King, and they are greatly sought after by rich men, because of Honour, Authoritie, and Power, which they have over others; but they may not sell, leave, nor resigne them.

One name.

All the Ilanders have but one name, without any sirname or name of the familie, and use frequently these names, Mahomet, Haly, Hussum, Assan, Ibrahim, and such others, but to know them, they distinguish them by their qualitie, which they adde in the end of their name as they that are of Noble race adde to their name Tacourou, and their Wives Bybis: Moreover they put also the Ile which is theirs. Those which are not Noble, but by their Office or qualitie, call themselves Callogues, and their Wives and Daughters, Camullogues. Not those onely which I have named use these, but others obtayning of the King vacant functions, to bee separated from the Plebeians. They buy this dearely of the King, because the Names and Titles are limited to a certayne number. The common people are called with their proper Callo, and adde also the trade and condition whereof they are, their Wives and Daughters Camulo. *Titles.* *Common people.*

The Palace of the King is built of Stone, composed of many handsome mansions and well built, yet without any ornament of Architecture, and of one storie. Round about it are Yardlands and Gardens, where are Fountaines and Cisternes of water, enclosed with walles and paved on the bottome with great smooth stones. These places are guarded continually by men appointed for it, because the King and Queenes wash themselves there, all others being straitly prohibited from washing there. In the inclosure of the Palace (called in their Language Gandoyre, which is very large) are many Lodgings and Courts, which have all in the midst a Well garnished with faire white stones. In one of these Courts, are two Magasins of the King: in one he puts his Ordnance, in the other all other sorts of Munition. *The Kings Palace.*

At the entrance of the Palace is a Corps de guard, where are many Pieces of Ordnance, and other kindes of Armes. The Portall is made like a square Tower, upon the top whereof on Feast dayes, players of Instruments play and sing. From thence they come to the first Hall, where the Souldiers wayte: a little further is another great Hall for the Signiors, Gentlemen, and persons of fashion. For none neither Signiors, nor Plebeian, man, woman, nor childe, dare goe further, except the domesticall Officers of *Guard.* *Two Halls.*

the King and Queenes, and their Slaves and Servitors. The pavement of these Hals are elevated three foot above the ground, and neatly boarded with wood well playned. It is thus raised up because of the Ants. Then the floore is after all covered with a little Matte, which they make in the Iles, interlaced in various colours, with Characters and other workes very finely contrived. The walls are hanged with Tapistrie of Silke; also upon the plat-fonds, it is covered with tapestrie of silke, from which hangs round about faire fringes as a Curtaine. The King made the great Ensigne and Banner of our ship which was blue,
[II.ix.1665.] where the Armes of France were well made, to bee displayed in the Souldiers and Strangers hall.

In these Halls before the place where the King sits, there is another forme of Curtaines very rich, under which is a large place elevated two foot, covered with a great Tapestrie, hereon they sit crosse-legged, for they use no other seats. Upon these Mattes throughout all the hall, the Nobles which come to assemble together sit downe. In this sitting they observe exactly the order of their Dignities: for they which are of lower degree, stay at the lower end, if the King or his Grandes which are there in his absence, bid them not sit. For the Gentlemen of the Ile of Male, and ordinarie Courtiers, which are bound to come and salute the King everie day after noone, stay and sit in the second Hall, and may goe no further, wayting till the King come foorth, or that they see some domesticke Officer, by whom they send the King word that they are come to salute him. Sometimes the King sends them while they are thus sitting, platters full of Bettell and Fruits, which they hold a great honour. The Gentrie of the other Ilands come also and observe the same customes that they doe of the Ile of Male: but they come
Presents. not without Presents, for none is permitted to salute the King, neither Noble-man nor Merchant, without one.

Chambers and Tapestrie. The Chambers and inner Lodgings are well adorned, hanged with Tapestrie of silke, inriched with flowers, boughes and branches of Gold, and of divers colours.

The people use tapestrie of Cotton, which is composed of many pieces of cloath of Cotton of all colours. Their Beds are hanged in the ayre by foure cords to a barre which is sustained with two pillers. They make the beds of the King and rich men in this sort, because they may rocke and shogge them more easily. They are accustomed when they are layd downe to make their folke touch and moove their bodie, and chafe them easily, strike them little blowes with both their hands together, saying that is good against the Spleene, and makes their griefe cease; also that it makes them sleepe soundly, and makes them forget the griefe of the member beaten and rubbed. *Beds.*

The ordinarie habillement of the King, is a white fine Robe of Cotton, or rather a Cassoque, descending to the girdle or a little lower, edged with white and blue, made fast before with massie buttons of Gold. With this he weares a piece of red imbroydered Taffetie, which reacheth from the girdle to the heele. This Taffetie is girded with a long large girdle of Silke fringed with Gold, and a great chayne of Gold before, whereat hangs a great Jewell as big as a hand, of exquisite stones which may bee seene. Hee weares also a knife after the manner of the Countrey, but more richly wrought. Upon his head hee hath a Bonnet of red Scarlet, which is much esteemed in this Countrey, and permitted to none but the King: this bonnet is laced with Gold, and on the top it hath a great button of massie Gold with a precious Stone; and although the Grandes and Souldiers weare their hayre long, yet hee hath his shaven every weeke. Hee useth to have his legges alwayes bare as others, and weares only on his feet Pantoffles of guilded Copper, brought out of Arabia and made like sandals. Of which sort none but the Queenes and Princesses his kinswomen may weare. When the King goeth foorth, hee hath a Sun-shadow or white Parosel, which is the principall Ensigne of Majestie, carryed over him. This is permitted to none but Strangers who may have what they will: alwayes there is one Page neere the King which carries a fanne, another the *Kings Robes.* *His bonnet and attire.* *Shaving.* *Bare legges.* *Ensignes of Majestie.*

Kings Sword and Buckler, another a boxe full of Betteli and Arecqua, which hee chawes every houre. A Doctor of the Law alwayes followes him, and never looseth sight of him, reading a Booke in his presence, and admonishing him of his Religion.

His Doctor.

His exercises and ordinarie pastimes are not to goe out and fish as his predecessors used to doe, but to remayne for the most immured in his Palace, to court his Queenes, see his Courtiers, and many Mechanickes and Artificers worke, as Painters, Goldsmiths, Imbroiderers, Cutlers, Joyners, Turners, Armorers, and others sorts which hee keepes in his Palace, and furnisheth them with matter to worke. Hee workes himselfe, and saith frequently that it is a sinne to bee idle. Hee hath a quicke and vive apprehension, and hath skill to worke in many Crafts and Mysteries, and is daily curious to learne: hee seekes out those which are excellent in any thing; if hee meet with any stranger that knowes that which he nor his Ilanders know not, he makes very much of him, that he may shew him his Art.

Exercises. *Workes.* *Respect of Arts.*

Going out of his Palace, hee is accompanied with his Souldiers, whereof hee hath a hundred every day for his Guard. On Friday he goeth to the Mosche, in a faire order and kind of pompe, for the Souldiers goe in rankes, some before and some behinde, and so his ordinarie Officers: the Drums, Flutes, Trumpets, make good agreeable musicke. After service is done, hee returnes in the same order, the Souldiers going with the sound of Instruments playing among them and leaping before the King with their armes, and striking blowes with their Swords on one anothers Bucklers: shewing their agilitie, yet not all together, to avoyde confusion but two at a time onely, and so one after another without ceasing. The people of the Ile which are present goe home with him, and it should bee a shame to any one not to goe. Then the Pandiare, Naybes, Catibes and Moüdins, and principall Signiors, Gentlemen and Souldiers, which hee chooseth diversly, dine with him, and after dinner hee imployes himselfe in

Guard and pompous going abroad.

doing Justice. Moreover, when the King goeth foorth hee is alwayes on foot (for in these Ilands is neither Horse nor any Beast to ride on) except hee bee carried in a Chayre on his Slaves shoulders: but this is seldome, because he is strong and lustie & had rather go on foot. When they speake to the King, or Queenes, and their Children and Princes of their bloud, or else if they speake of them to others, it is in other termes which they use not but for this, and dare not apply them to others. As if they say of a man hee sleepeth, if it bee of the King, they say, he slumbreth or takes his rest, which they never say but speaking of the King.

No Beast to ride on.

[II.ix.1666.]

Complement.

The Queenes are attired as other women formerly described, but in more costly manner. The Ladies, Wives and Daughters of the Grand Signiors of the Ile, are bound to come see them in the evening, to passe the time with them. They goe sometimes forth, but it is very rare: and then there are women and slaves which goe a great way before, to advertise the men that they retire and appeare not in the way, but onely the women, who assemble by their quarters and divisions, and come to meet them with Presents of Flowers and Fruits. There are foure principall women which carry over the Queenes head a white Curtine of Silke reaching to the ground, so that they cannot be seene. They goe often to bath in the Sea, as all other women: for it is the custome of the Country, and they hold it very healthfull; for this cause therefore they have prepared in the Sea a little inclosure, covered round with Cotton cloth, where the Queenes and great women bath: after they come out they have another little house also made purposely where they bath againe in Fresh-water. Within the chambers of the Queenes, Princesses, and great Ladies they never see day, nor have any other light but of Lamps, which burne continually. They retyre themselves into a part of the chamber, being enclosed with foure or five rowes of Tapistry, which they must lift up before they come where they are: but none neither man nor woman, domesticall nor others dare lift

Queenes, and their pompe.

Bathing in the salt and fresh-water.

Perpetuall night.

up the hindmost, although they are not laid, nor eating, in briefe although they be idle. They must first cough, and tell who they be, and then they call them or send them whither they thinke good. Neither women nor maids pull off the cloth which goes about their middle, but only their robe: the men doe so also, and dare not doe otherwise.

Revenues. The Kings revenewes consists in his Crownelands, which are many Ilands; and the duties which his subjects pay of the fruits which grow in the Countrie, that is to say, the fifth part of the graines which they sow, they give the King a portion of their Cocos and Limons, they compound also throughout all the yeere for a certaine quantitie of Hony or fruit. Besides these duties the King *Al paid in kind.* imposeth an ordinary taxe on his subjects, according to their meanes, which consists in cords of Cocos, in shells called Boly, and dryed Fish. For they give him no mony for his Taxes and Rents, but onely when they buy Titles and Offices, and have permission to weare their braveries. Also hee chargeth the Inhabitants of the Iles to make and *Cotton clothes.* furnish him yeerely Cotton clothes, which serveth him for his Souldiers, to whom hee gives thrice a yeere Cloth, besides their pay. The revenew of the King consists also *Merchandise.* in merchandise: For all the Ships which arrive there, first goe to him, and declare what they have brought, after they agree to a certaine price for that which hee will have, which is very often the better part: after the people buy it at a dearer rate then the King; and then the King sends to distribute his merchandise throughout the Iles to the richest, at what price hee will; although they have no use of it, taking in exchange such merchandise, as hee hath need of, at a better price by halfe then it is worth. He sends often also Ships laden with merchandise of his Ile to other Countries. The King hath also besides these *Wrackes.* Royalties, whatsoever is found on the Sea shoare, and no man dare touch it to detaine it, but is bound to take it up and bring it him, whether it bee pieces of shipwrackt Ships, pieces of Wood, Coffers, or other things: or Amber

Greece, which they call Gomen, hereof is the greatest quantitie in the Indies, and none dare keepe it on paine of having his hand cut off.

Also there is a certaine Nut, which the Sea sometimes casts up, which is as great as a mans head: they call it Tauarcarre, and suppose that it commeth of certaine trees that are under the sea: the Portugals call them Cocos of the Maldives. It is a thing very medicinable & of great price. Also the fishing for Blacke Corrall appertaines to the King, who hath many men to make this fishing. The mony of the Kingdome is onely Silver, and of one kind. These are pieces of Silver which they call Larins, of the valew of eight Sols or thereabouts of our mony, long as a finger, but much folded. The King coynes them in his Iland, and imprints on them his name in Arabick letters. The other monyes are Exotick coynes, and there goe currant, but they take them not but at just value, and at equall weights, and onely the Gold or Silver, all other sorts of coyne which are not of the Countrie they reject. For in India, as there are many Realmes and Signiories, so great diversitie of mony, of stampe and character, not onely of Gold and Silver, but also of an other mettall called Calin, which is white like Tin, and very hard, pure, and beautifull, whereof they make great esteeme in the Indies; they have also Iron mony. But this kind of mony goeth onely in the Dominions of the Prince that coynes it. The Gold and Silver of whatsoever stampe and character it be, is currant through all Kingdomes according to the just valew, which is of different valew from ours, because Silver is deerer then here, and Gold baser. The King makes no lesser coynes then the Larin: so that to effect their merchandise, they cut the Silver and give in weight according to the valew of the merchandise: which is not without losse, for in cutting of a Larin they lose the twelfth part. They take no piece of Silver which they have not weighed, and put in the fire to try the goodnesse: every one hath weights in his house for this purpose. Also in stead of little and base mony they

Sea Nuts. *Coyne.* *Buying.*

use shells, whereof 12000. goe at the valew of a Larin.
[II.ix.1667.] All their Gold and Silver come from forraine places, for they have no coine in these Iles. In all their publique markets and particuler bargainings, they use to exchange very often one thing for another.

Bartering.

Merchants.

The Maldives are very well frequented with Merchants of many Countries, as of the Malabares, of Barcelor, Onor, Bacalor, Cananor, Calecut, Tananor, Cochin, Coulam, Cael: of the Guzerattes, of Cambaia, Surate, and Chaule of the Arabs, Persians, of those of Bengale, Saint Thomæ and Masulipatan, Ceylan and Sumatra; which bring Merchandise whereof the Ilanders have need and esteeme, and in recompence carrie away those things wherewith the Ilands abound. First of the Cocos tree, they make many kindes of things, which the strangers seeke after, as Cordage, wherewith they trim all the Ships of the Indies: they lade yeerely more then one hundred ships of the fruit of the Cocos, which they carry into the Coasts of Arabia, Malabar, and throughout all India, also Oyle and Honey of the same Tree: and weaving the Leaves of this tree serve them to make Sayles.

Merchandise.

Coco commodities.

Shell money.

There is another sort of riches in the Ilands: These are little shells wherein there is a little creature, as great as the end of the little finger, all white, very smooth and glistering, which they fish for but twice a moneth, three dayes before, and three dayes after the new Moone, and likewise the Full, and finde them at no other season. The women gather them upon the sands and flats of the Sea, being in the water to the girdle. They transport great quantities of them to other Countries, insomuch that I have seene yeerely thirtie or fortie ships laden without any other commoditie. They goe all into Bengala: for there onely they buy them at great prices, and in great quantitie. They of Bengala make such esteeme of them, that they use them as common money, although they have Gold and Silver, and enough of other mettals: and that which is more marvellous, the Kings and Nobles build places to lay them up in, and account them part of their

Treasure. They give twentie * measures of Rice for one fardell of Shels. For all these Bolys are put up by fardels of twelve thousand together in little baskets made of the Cocos leafe, garnished within with cloath made of the same Tree, for feare the shells should fall out. They much esteeme in India Tortois shells, which they call Cambe. This sort of Tortois is found no where but there, and in the Philippinas: it is faire, very smooth, all blacke, with very naturall figures. They sell them best in Cambaia where they make (besides bracelets for women) faire Coffers and Cabbinets inlayed with silver. They make heere very fine mattes of Reed of divers colours, and inrich them with ornaments and ciphers very neatly. They have also faire cloaths of Cotton and Silke.

*Coquettes.

Tortoys shells.

In counter-change of these the Merchants bring them Rice, white Cotton clothes, and cloath of Silke: Oyle which is made of an odoriferous Graine, wherewith they use to rub their bodies when they have bathed, Arecqua, Iron and Steele, Spices, Porcelane, and whatsoever they have need of: and yet every thing is very cheape by reason of the abundance, and ordinarie arrivall of Ships. They bring also Gold and Silver, which never goeth foorth againe: for they give it not for any thing to Strangers, but put it among the Treasure and Jewels of their Wives.

Exotike wares.

§. VI.

A larger discourse of their Religion, manifold Ceremonies, and absurd opinions. The Authors departure and returne.

THeir Religion is Mahometan, their Temples or Moschees are builded square of hewen stone. They have three doores, and at the entrie of each doore on the outside, there is a large Well whereinto they descend by degrees, the bottomes and sides are garnished with polished stone, in these they use to bathe themselves.

Moschees.

The Temple is elevated nine or ten greeces; the floore of it is covered with Mattes and Tapistrie: they are very curious to keepe them neate and handsome; they dare not spit in them, nor blow their nose, but if they bring no handkerchiffe with them, if they have any necessitie, they must goe foorth. The roofe is of wood, of excellent Carpenters worke, the wall waynscotted, whereon hang Tables of wood or stone, engraven with letters and writings in Arabicke. There are separations of certaine places appointed to certaine persons, yet not to one particuler person, but for those which are of one order, estate, age, or qualitie, and none dare place himselfe in a place not appointed for his condition. Within the Temples are Lamps light continually. Every Mosche hath a Moudin or Priest. Each day in the weeke, they goe at the breake of day to the Mosche, and there make a prayer according to their beliefe, that is to say, that the world is flat and not round, and that there is a wall of Copper about it, which hinders the world from being overwhelmed with the waters which invirone it, and that the Devill the enemy of Mankinde, seekes every night to pierce thorow and undermine this wall, and by day breake hee wants very little to have made a hole thorow; for this cause all the men from fifteene yeeres old, goe at the point of day to their Moschees, to make prayers, saying that without their prayers all the world would perish.

Order.

Lights and darkenesse.

Their beliefe of the world, the Devill and their Prayers.

[II.ix.1668.]

Five times a day praying.

Women-recusants.

They goe foure other times in a day to the Mosche: at mid-day, three houres after, at Sun-set, and ten a clocke in the evening, and tarie each time halfe an houre. The Women never enter into their Temples, but abide in their houses, and there make Prayers. Yet if they goe not to their Temples the ordinarie dayes of the weeke, they make their Prayers and Ceremonies in their houses or else-where: and although they constraine none to doe thus; yet if they know of any that neglects it, they will neither eate nor communicate with them. Before they enter into the Temple, they wash their feete, hands, eares, mouth, and eyes, making also certaine Ceremonies, and pronouncing prayers, which are divers according to the houres, feasts, occasions, for which they wash. If they

Washing rites.

Diversified devotions.

make urine, or doe their necessities, or touch their privities, they wash and say their prayers destined for that: If they have accompanied with a woman, they must bath and say their Prayers of another sort; if with their owne wife, of another sort. They wash and bath in publike and say their prayers so loude, that by the diversitie of prayers according to the occasions, a man may know what they have done in secret, and when they have lyen with their wives, or else with others.

They are all Circumcised, the males at seven yeere old. *Circumcision.* Before an Infant is Circumcised, they say hee is an Innocent, and cannot sinne. For their Daughters, they make *Females.* no feasts nor ceremonies, but for their Circumcision draw two or three drops of blood from their nature, then when they come to the age of ten yeeres old. All the yeere long they celebrate many Feasts. First everie weeke they *Feasts.* solemnize Friday. On Thursday in the evening, some make prayers for their health, others for the deceased: and therefore they prepare to eate and drinke, and send to their Priests or Moudins neere the place where their dead are interred, to pray to God for them: or else they invite them to their houses, and there entertaine them. On Friday morning one goeth through the Ile carrying in his hand a kind of cast Bell, much *Bells.* resembling the cover of a Limbeck, with a hammer of wood, wherewith hee beates it: and at the end of everie street hee stayes, and admonisheth the people, that is their feast Oucourou or Friday. Hee is assisted with three persons which have straight Trumpets, wherewith they *Trumpets.* often sound. The people being thus warned cease from their worke, and bathe and wash themselves, saying their Prayers. And each of them cloathes himselfe in his best attire, and all from the age of fifteene yeeres are bound to bee there. In the meane while on the portall of the Kings Palace, are players of divers Instruments. Then the Kings *Holiday sute and service.* foure Moudins all together ascend an Edifice or stone, high erected, joyning to the Mosche, putting their hands to their eares, crying thrice with all their might with a most fearefull voice all together in the Arabicke language, Alas, alas Aquebar, that is to say, Great God: and then they adde something of Mahomet.

Their Office or rites of service.

Then they goe to the Kings Palace; and the King, if hee will bee found, as hee is seldome defective, sends a Carpet of silke to spread in the place where he will sit: if hee doth not, it is a certaine signe hee will not bee found. When all the companie is assembled (and the King is come and hath made his prayers) the Catibe ascends a raised place of wood sixe or seven steppes high. There hee holds a naked Sword in his hand, with the point downward, which hee often flourisheth this way and that way, and recites his prayers. All this time the people pray without ceasing, putting themselves in divers postures, sitting, standing upright, kneeling, their face grovelling to the earth, their hands lifted up and cast downe, then crossed, turning their head and eyes hither and thither: it were very difficult to represent all the gestures and apish tricks which they doe in this time: then they put off their weapons, and their knives, and dare have nothing about them but their cloathes, and they also must bee very neate. The Catibe changeth his prayers every Friday to the end of the yeere, and then begins againe. Hee saith all by heart, and in the meane time one of the Moudins holds the Booke, and if it chanceth that hee faileth in one word, sillable, or letter, the Moudine reprehends him with a loud voyce and without dissembling: for they say, if hee should faile in one point, the Feast should bee nullified, and worth nothing.

Divers gestures and postures.

Service by heart.

New Moone rites.

On the dayes of their New Moone all the yeere long, they make the like Feast, and rejoyce when they see the new Moone: then they make cleane their Houses, Courts, and all their streets and the wayes to the Mosches, and all the gates of their houses as well without as within, and they set on both sides Cocos shells cut in the middle, like woodden dishes, and fill them with white sand, and burning coales upon it, scarce ceasing all the night to burne Aromaticke gummes, and odoriferous woods and perfumes: likewise within in their Houses, at the corners of their

Beds and else-where, they besmeare and fashion all their doores and housholdstuffe at their feasts, with Sanders, and other sweet smelling odours beaten and tempered together; but above all, they solemnise foure New Moones in the yeere more then the others. *Sweet smells.*

In the moneth of December or thereabouts at the New Moone, they observe a feast called in Arabicke Ramedan: this begins at the new Moone, and ends at the new Moone following. This night the men and the women each by themselves visite one another, and feast, and rejoyce together with banquets, dances and merriments, so that it is neere day before they retire. The day before, they bathe and make particuler ceremonies, cleanse and wash their teeth, and leave their Bettell, and thence forward fast till night although the day be long, with such superstition, that they will not only not taste any thing, but also not wash their mouth, nor put their fingers in it, nor yet swallow their spittle. This causeth them often to spit, and diseaseth them much, especially at their Mesquit, where it is not lawfull for them to spit, but ever and anone they must goe forth for that purpose. The men may wash themselves * but not plunge their heads in water, lest some drop should enter their mouthes or eares: but the women dare not, lest the water should enter at their lower parts. Halfe an houre before Sunne-set, all which are fifteene yeeres old and upwards goe to the Temple, that they may in that halfe houres space cleanse their mouthes and picke their teeth very exactly; to which purpose the Moudins furnish themselves all the Lent with Pick-tooths, and other instruments of neatnesse, made of the Coco wood. This done, the Moudin makes his crie three times, and enters the Temple; all the People are behinde him; thus they make their Prayers there, and the women in their houses; which ended, they make good cheere with their friends, and feast each other by course, having made provision long before to that end; the poorest sparing before hand that they may have to feast during the Ramedan. The King makes severall entertainments,

Foure principall New Moones.
Ramedan.
Severe fasting.
[II.ix.1669.]
**S. Augustin in divers places mentions the Christians of those parts of Africa in his time, not washing till the Fast were ended.*
Feast-fasts.

one day feasting his Nobles, another his Souldiers, a third the Pandeare, Moudins and Religious persons; and all the people of the Ile in their differing rankes. The Nobles observe the like custome for their friends and equals; for they religiously observe this, not to eate with men of differing ranke and qualitie. Men and Boyes feast thus, the Women goe not, but send Presents and Viands one to another, and bathe themselves in the evening, at which time, men may not bee admitted to bathe. In the day-time the men neither marrie nor touch their women: and during the Ramedan they are more carefull to avoide sinne then at other times. And if any by occasion breakes any of the Fasting-dayes, hee fasteth as many after; which often happeneth by reason of their superstition, supposing their Fast defective, if they happe to bleed in any part. They will not in this moneth worke, be they never so poore, nor travell or send out of their Ile.

Ridiculous Fast-breaches and making amends.

Daily Sermons.

The Pandiare (whom the Arabs call the Cadi) every day preacheth at the Kings Palace, or at the Temple, or at his House, beginning at three after noone, and holding on two houres; and all the Inhabitants of the Ile of Malé assemble thither: this commonly in the vulgar Language, and sometimes in Arabike, which hee after interpreteth. They employ themselves the rest of the time in exercise of Armes and divers playes, as at the Ball, in severall companies, with their feet: the women and daughters also have their visitations and petie sports. The youths also and maidens court and make love to each other more in that moneth then at other times; send each other Songs, Sonnets, and Verses written in Coco leaves (which are as white as Paper) inscribed or graven with Bodkins; and send Garlands of the fairest and sweetest flowers to their Sweet-hearts. All devise pastimes to entertaine that moneth. The women and maidens for their flowers sake must fast eight dayes more then the men, after the Ramedan is ended.

Love-moneth.

Three dayes before it ends, the Coly warneth all from

the top of the Steeple to send their names to the Pandiare of Malé, as in other Ilands to the Naybe, to pay their offerings (halfe a Larin for each person) or else man and boy, woman and maide have lost the merite of their fasting, saying it is their Tribute to God and Mahomet. They which have it not may borrow, for the King and the richer sort will pay for all that aske; but if any will not indure the shame that another should pay for him, his name is recorded neverthelesse, and he makes it his debt, to pay after the feast. Parents pay for their children till they be married and dwell from them, as also for their slaves. This money is after divided into three parts: and foure Receivers are appointed, one on behalfe of the King, another for the Church-men, the third for New Converts, the fourth for the Poore: there are eight Registers which record the offerings. It is after shared one part to the Priests, as the Pandiare, Naybes, Catibes, Moudins, Devanits, and others of their Church: The second to the Converts, the third to the Poore. On the last day of the Fast is celebrated a great Feast called Ydu. The day is no more certaine then the beginning of the Ramedan, which is when they first see the New Moone, as in all their Moon-feasts, not at the change but at the appearance, which is therefore sooner or later in one Iland then another, as it hath had cleerer weather or sooner sight. Their May Ydu, a three dayes solemnitie; and their Poycacan at the Full Moone about Aprill or May; and their Dida, or All-Soules feast in June, when they visit the Sepulchres and there set viands; and their Candis Cacan in August; and Maulude or Night-feast in October (the night that Mahomet died) with the severall ceremonies thereof, as also of their Marriages and Funerals, I dare not present you for feare of tediousnesse.

Halfe a Larin, a generall personal offering, as halfe a shekel amongst the Israelites.

No New moon feast certaine. They ascend high places purposely being ambitious every man of her first sight.

Wee will therefore returne with our Authour, and free you also from the Maldives. Tenne dayes before his libertie he had a dreame that hee was free and in Christendome, whereat hee much rejoyced, and awaking made a Vow to make a Voyage to S. James of Galicia, to give God

Bengalan Fleet. In February. 1607.

thankes. Two nights after the King was told of an Armada of sixteene Gallies or Galliots comming thither. The King commanded to rigge his seven Gallies with other Ships, Barkes and Boates. This was attempted with all industrie, but could not be effected before the Enemies Fleet came in sight. Thereupon he charged that all his
[II.ix.1670.] best goods should be embarqued, so to save himselfe and his women in the Southerne Iles. He forsooke his Palace, and fled with his three Queenes, each of them carried in armes by Gentlemen, as Nurses carrie their Infants; covered with Vailes and Taffataes of divers colours. The streets were full of cries of women and infants. He was forced to leave great part of his goods and all his Armes and Ordnance behind for want of time; and with much lamentation set sayle for the South, to the Atollons of Souadou. But the winde fayled, and the Enemie sent eight Gallies after him, in fight with whom the King was slaine, and his wives and goods taken. The other eight entred on land, and the Authour yeelded to them, and being found not to be a Portugall, was spared. They stayd ten dayes to lade their Gallies with the goods which they found, and with five or sixe score peeces of Ordnance great and small (a principall cause of their Voyage) and then departed, leaving the Queenes and all the people in libertie, except the brother of the Chiefe Queene and the Kings brother in law. His arrivall in Malicut a small Ile, and the Iles Divandurou thirty leagues thence, and at last at Chatigan in Bengala, I omit. At his departure from Bengala, the Mogol had denounced warre to the chiefe King of Bengala, who prepared to entertaine him with above a million of men and ten thousand Elephants. The Kings of Aracan and Chaul, and other great Lords, Mahumetans and Gentiles were his Tributaries, and were bound to finde him a certaine number of men and horses. The successe is related by others, and other things many of many other Indian Regions are related by the Authour, whom wee are willing now to dismisse, having entertained him only for a Maldivan Guide and Pilot.

Bengalans hate the Portugals.

Mogols conquest of Bengala. See in Capt. Hawkins and S. Thomas Roe.

The particulars of his returne he relateth at large: first his passage from Bengala to Movtingué, governed by a petie Prince, a Nairo, subject to the Samory of Calecut. It is seated betwixt Cananor and Calecut, and is a Port of the Malabar Pirats. He was here much amazed to see so many in Armes, borne by all from ten or twelve yeeres. There are ten other neere Ports within ten small leagues of each other, Chombais, Badara, &c. But Moutingué is the best. Thence he went to Calicut and waiting eight moneths for a Holland ship in vaine, he was perswaded by Jesuites to goe to Cochin, where he was imprisoned for a Spie. At Goa also hee was prisoner with those which remained of the seventeene Englishmen taken at the Barre of Surrat. The Jesuits had brought one Master Richard and foure other Englishmen from the Mogols Court; some Hollanders also were there: and they all were prisoners together. But the Jesuites undertooke for them, and procured their libertie; namely Thomas Stevens an Englishman, Rector of Margon Colledge in Salsete, and Nicolas Trigaut a Wallon, and Steven Crosse a Frenchman of Roan, with Gaspar Aleman a Spaniard. The said Thomas Stevens procured the libertie of the Englishmen also, foure of which became Catholike-Romanists, and two of them died there. Don Loys Lorencio d'Establa arrived at Goa with the title of Vice-roy, to the peoples great griefe, which more desired Don André Furtado. Ten moneths after his comming, foure great Caracks arrived, contayning each about two thousand tunnes. Five had departed from Lisbon, but they knew not what was becomne of the fift, separated by tempest at the Cape. In each were embarqued a thousand persons, Souldiers, Mariners, Jesuites, and other Church-men, with Merchants and Gentlemen. But when they arrived at Goa, there were not above three hundred in each, by reason of sicknesse and miseries endured eight moneths at Sea, without sight of Land. These brought an Edict from the King, forbidding English, French, or Dutch commerce, and if there were any such there, to packe them away upon perill

Movtingué.

See sup. in Hawkins and Fitches Voyages. pagg. 207. 420.

Thomas Stevens an English Jesuite which had long continued there.

Kings Edict (in effect) to roote out the Portugals from the Indies, enjoyning and not enabling to warre with others.

of their lives. On the sixe and twentieth of December, 1609. He returned for Lisbon. March the fifteenth, 1610, they arrived at the Ile of Diego Rodrigue, in 20. Southerne degrees, about forty leagues East from Saint Laurence. After a cruell storme there five dayes together, they attained the Cape, Saint Helena, Brasill, the Acores, the Berlings, and having payed his vow to Saint James in Galicia, he arrived at Rochell, the sixteenth of Februarie, 1611.

The end of the ninth Booke.

END OF VOLUME IX.